MELVILLE'S FOLK ROOTS

Melville's Folk Roots

KEVIN J. HAYES

THE KENT STATE UNIVERSITY PRESS

Kent, Ohio, & London

© 1999 by The Kent State University Press, Kent, Ohio 44242
Library of Congress Catalog Card Number 98-45710
ISBN 0-87338-625-6
Manufactured in the United States of America

05 04 03 02 01 00 99   5 4 3 2 1

Library of Congress Cataloging-in-Publication Data
Hayes, Kevin J.

    Melville's folk roots / Kevin J. Hayes.

       p.   cm.

    Includes bibliographical references (p.   ) and index.

    ISBN 0-87338-625-6 (cloth : alk. paper) ∞

    1. Melville, Herman, 1819–1891—Knowledge—Folklore.
2. Literature and folklore—United States—History—19th century.
3. Oral tradition—United States. 4. Folklore in literature.
I. Title.
PS2388.F64H39   1999
813'.3—dc21   98-45710

British Library Cataloging-in-Publication data are available.

For my parents

Contents

Preface

When Fletcher S. Bassett assembled *Legends and Superstitions of the Sea* in 1885, he cited several of Herman Melville's works to illustrate different aspects of nautical folklore. He cited *Moby-Dick* not only for whaling legends but also in his discussions of the luminous phenomenon known as St. Elmo's Fire and the omens associated with seals' cries and other mysterious sounds at sea. Furthermore, Bassett footnoted *White-Jacket,* mentioned the story of spontaneous combustion from *Redburn* in his treatment of traditional stories containing similar motifs, and elsewhere referred to "The Encantadas." The multiple references show that Bassett was among the few who read and appreciated Melville during the 1880s. Needless to say, Melville's reputation went through a metamorphosis over the next several decades, during which he received his due recognition as a great writer. Though enthusiasm for Melville continues to grow, those who have appreciated his use of folklore remain few.

Literary appreciation for Melville's use of folklore began with Constance Rourke's *American Humor: A Study of the National Character.* Rourke, like those who have extended the study of Melville's humor, such as Edward Rosenberry, Jane Mushabac, and John Bryant, made broad generalizations about Melville's tall-tale humor, yet even she gave little attention to his specific borrowings from the oral tradition. Starting with Richard Chase's *Herman Melville: A Critical Study,* scholars began to scrutinize Melville's use of folklore more closely. After Chase, Daniel Hoffman devoted separate chapters to *Moby-Dick* and *The Confidence-Man* in *Form and Fable in American Fiction,* and Janez Stanonik examined Melville's debt to whaling lore in *Moby Dick: The Myth and the Symbol, A Study in Folklore and Literature.* Both Chase and Hoffman associated Melville's *Confidence-Man* with the traditional Yankee huckster, an interpretation which Johannes Dietrich Bergmann largely rendered out of date with his discovery of the original confidence man. To be sure, *The Confidence-Man* owes a debt to folklore, but its use of folk speech, especially proverbs, now seems more important than its use of traditional character types. Discussing *Moby-Dick*, Hoffman paid less attention to the work's folklore and more attention to Melville's use of classical mythology. Though better than most, Hoffman's application of mythic criticism was by no means unusual, for numerous academic critics in the late 1950s and early 1960s used the approach to study other literary works. Separate essays identifying mythical patterns in *Redburn, White-Jacket,* and *Pierre* appeared in due course. The finest treatment of Melville and myth remains H. Bruce Franklin's *The Wake of the Gods*.

The present study is *not* a study of Melville's use of classical mythology. I am less interested in what Melville might have read in his copy of Harpers' *Classical Library* than what he *heard* from his friends, family members, shipmates, and fellow patrons of the barbershop and the tavern. What oral traditions did Melville know? How did he incorporate them into his writing? This study seeks answers to such questions.

The first five chapters are devoted to different folk genres. Though the last three chapters are devoted to individual works—*Redburn, Moby-Dick,* and *Clarel*—each relates to a specific folk genre as well. In the first five chapters, I range freely among Melville's works. In one paragraph I may be aboard the *Julia* with Dr. Long Ghost; another may find me lurking about Saddle Meadows with Pierre Glendinning; in the next I may be on the road from Jerusalem to the Dead Sea with Clarel. While I assume my readers are generally familiar with Melville's books, it is not essential to have read all of them to follow this one. I have tried to give enough background information to allow initiates to read with ease, yet not so much as to weary seasoned Melville scholars. This work has been designed for a wide readership: undergraduates taking their first survey course in American literature, graduate students, Melville scholars, folklorists, or anyone who appreciates Melville's writings and enjoys learning more about the man and his work. Though this book specifically concentrates on Melville's use of folklore, it also serves as a general overview of his writings.

Chapter 1, "Superstition and the Sea," discusses how Melville used sailor superstitions in his writings. This chapter comes first, for as

Melville well recognized, other folk genres, especially legends, often built upon superstitions. Understanding how Melville used superstition, therefore, is helpful for understanding how he used other types of folklore.

Melville's adaptation of folksongs has received a fair amount of attention over the past several decades. In the mid-1950s, Paul Clayton assembled and recorded several traditional songs and released the LP *Whaling and Sailing Songs from the Days of Moby Dick*. In the mid-1960s, Agnes Dicken Cannon contributed a fine article discussing Melville's use of sea shanties, ballads, and songs. Less than a decade later, Robert J. Schwendinger discussed the influence of the sea shanty on Melville's diction. In the next decade, Stuart M. Frank discussed sea shanties in *Omoo* and *Moby-Dick*. Ray Browne reminds us, however, that despite these fine treatments more work remains to be done on Melville's use of folksongs. Chapter 2, "Fiction and Folksong," extends the work of earlier scholars, looking specifically at how Melville blended oral verse with prose text as he used plots from narrative songs and the emotional associations of others to enhance his fiction. Since the focus of this chapter is Melville's prose fiction, I reserve my brief discussion of *Clarel*'s debt to the traditional ballad for Chapter 8.

Merton Babcock pioneered the study of Melville's proverbs and folk speech during the early 1950s, and Archer Taylor and Bartlett Jere Whiting catalogued many of his proverbs in the late 1950s. Since then, Melville's use of proverbs has scarcely attracted scholarly attention. Chapter 3, "Proverb and Irony," attempts to analyze how the traditional sayings Melville incorporated in his works function, both rhetorically and aesthetically. As the chapter's title indicates, Melville often used proverbs for ironic purposes. In a small way, this chapter extends and supplements John Seelye's fine critical study, *Melville: The Ironic Diagram*.

Chapter 4, "Phantom Sailors," is the first of several chapters devoted to folk narrative. The folk genre it treats is the personal legend commonly known as the ghost story. Instead of simply analyzing Melville's ghost stories, however, I look specifically at how several different folk genres—burial customs, superstitions, personal narratives, tales, and legends—come together in performance.

Though Melville ranks among American literature's best tall-tale tellers, his use of the tall tale has gone largely unappreciated outside of humor studies. Some years ago Bartlett C. Jones published a brief article that identified several tall tales in *Typee,* and more recently Neil Grobman has analyzed Melville's use of tall tales in *Moby-Dick;* otherwise, however, students of the tall tale have ignored Melville. The fullest study of the tall tale in America, Carolyn S. Brown's *The Tall Tale in American Folklore and Literature,* analyzes its function in both social and literary contexts, yet Brown ignores Melville in her general survey of American literature. In Chapter 5, "Tall Talk and Tall Tales," I correct Brown's oversight by applying her analysis of the tall tale to Melville's fiction.

Despite Merton M. Sealts's authoritative treatment of Melville's reading and Mary Kay Bercaw's fine study of his sources, Melville's debt to the chapbook remains largely unstudied. Such neglect is not unique to Melville scholarship, for the chapbook often falls between the two stools of literary history and folklore studies. Though some chapbooks contain traditional narratives and others list occult practices, folklorists sometimes ignore them because they are printed works; literary historians, on the other hand, see the chapbook as a sub-literary genre not worth serious study. Though Melville did not use the term "chapbook" in his published writings, he did speak of cheap pamphlets, paperbound occult books, children's story books, and popular literature, all of which more or less fit under the general term. Chapter 6, "*Redburn* and the Chapbook," examines the relationship of the popular book to Melville's work, using *Redburn* as an example. The chapter also examines his comments about the popular book in *Mardi* and makes some conjectures about what chapbooks Melville read in his youth.

In *Herman Melville: A Biography,* Hershel Parker suggested that Melville's lengthy return journey from England in early 1850 gave him ample opportunity to brood about the book he would write next, the one that would follow *White-Jacket.* In England he had considered rewriting the story of Israel Potter, yet not long after reaching home he began writing a story based on whaling legend, the work that would become *Moby-Dick.* In the first half of Chapter 7, "*Moby-Dick,* Legend in the Making," I provide some surmises about why Melville's interests shifted from the story of Israel Potter to the whaling legend during that long shipboard brooding. The second half of the chapter looks specifically at how he shaped a legend originally told among sailors into a literary tale for "fireside people."

Chapter 8, "Legend, Belief, Tradition, and *Clarel*," also takes up the legend genre, looking specifically at Christian legends, stories that Melville had undoubtedly heard in his family during his childhood and, just as undoubtedly, resented as a young adult. This chapter examines how Melville's wider understanding of legend—South Pacific, ancient Greek, or Christian—combined with his journey to the Holy Land, allowed him to appreciate Christian legend and eventually to make literary use of it.

By way of conclusion, I return to sailor folklore to analyze briefly one of Melville's late volumes of poetry, *John Marr and Other Sailors, with Some Sea-Pieces,* a work which shows that though Melville sometimes treated sailor superstitions sarcastically, he nevertheless retained fond memories of traditions he had learned a half-century before.

THANKS GO OUT TO SEVERAL people. Susan Spencer provided helpful information for Chapter 8. Hershel Parker read an early draft of the manuscript and suggested several improvements, many of which I have incorporated. I also thank Parker for directing my attention to Gansevoort Melville's *Index Rerum* at the Berkshire Athenaeum in Pittsfield, Massachusetts, and I am grateful to the Athenaeum for allowing me to reprint excerpts from Gansevoort's manuscript entries in his *Index Rerum.* I would also like to thank those who read the manuscript for The Kent State University Press as well as Julia J. Morton and the staff of The Kent State University Press for their help. Finally, I thank my parents for their encouragement and support from the beginning.

Abbreviations

AT   Aarne, Antti, and Stith Thompson. *The Types of the Folktale: A Classification and Bibliography . . . Second Revision*. Helsinki: Suomalainen Tiedeakatemia Academia Scientarum Fennica, 1961.

BB   Melville, Herman. *Billy Budd, Sailor: An Inside Narrative*. Ed. Harrison Hayford and Merton M. Sealts, Jr. Chicago: University of Chicago, 1962.

Cl   ———. *Clarel: A Poem and Pilgrimage in the Holy Land*. Ed. Harrison Hayford, Alma A. MacDougall, Hershel Parker, and G. Thomas Tanselle. Evanston and Chicago: Northwestern University Press and The Newberry Library, 1991.

CM   ———. *The Confidence-Man: His Masquerade*. Ed. Harrison Hayford, Hershel Parker, and G. Thomas Tanselle. Evanston and Chicago: Northwestern University Press and The Newberry Library, 1984.

Co   ———. *Correspondence*. Ed. Lynn Horth. Evanston and Chicago: Northwestern University Press and The Newberry Library, 1993.

CP   ———. *Collected Poems of Herman Melville*. Ed. Howard P. Vincent. Chicago: Hendricks House, 1947.

IP   ———. *Israel Potter: His Fifty Years of Exile*. Ed. Harrison Hayford, Hershel Parker, and G. Thomas Tanselle. Evanston and Chicago: Northwestern University Press and The Newberry Library, 1982.

J   ———. *Journals*. Ed. Howard C. Horsford and Lynn Horth. Evanston and Chicago: Northwestern University Press and The Newberry Library, 1989.

M   ———. *Mardi and a Voyage Thither*. Ed. Harrison Hayford, Hershel Parker, and G. Thomas Tanselle. Evanston and Chicago: Northwestern University Press and The Newberry Library, 1970.

MD   ———. *Moby-Dick: Or, The Whale*. Ed. Harrison Hayford, Hershel Parker, and G. Thomas Tanselle. Evanston and Chicago: Northwestern University Press and The Newberry Library, 1988.

motif   Thompson, Stith. *Motif-Index of Folk-Literature: A Classification of Narrative Elements in Folktales, Ballads, Myths, Fables, Mediaeval Romances, Exempla, Fabliaux, Jest-Books, and Local Legends*. Rev. ed. 6 vols. Bloomington: Indiana University Press, 1955–58.

O   Melville, Herman. *Omoo: A Narrative of Adventures in the South Seas*. Ed. Harrison Hayford, Hershel Parker, and G. Thomas Tanselle. Evanston and Chicago: Northwestern University Press and The Newberry Library, 1968.

PT   ———. *The Piazza Tales and Other Prose Pieces, 1839–1860*. Ed. Harrison Hayford, Alma A. MacDougall, and G. Thomas Tanselle. Evanston and Chicago: Northwestern University Press and The Newberry Library, 1987.

R   ———. *Redburn: His First Voyage, Being the Sailor-Boy Confessions and Reminiscences of the Son-of-a-Gentleman, in the Merchant Service*. Ed. Harrison Hayford, Hershel Parker, and G. Thomas Tanselle. Evanston and Chicago: Northwestern University Press and The Newberry Library, 1969.

T   ———. *Typee: A Peep at Polynesian Life*. Ed. Harrison Hayford, Hershel Parker, and G. Thomas Tanselle. Evanston and Chicago: Northwestern University Press and The Newberry Library, 1968.

WJ   ———. *White-Jacket: Or, The World in a Man-of-War*. Ed. Harrison Hayford, Hershel Parker, and G. Thomas Tanselle. Evanston and Chicago: Northwestern University Press and The Newberry Library, 1970.

Superstition and
the Sea

*J*ulia, the barque Herman Melville imagined for *Omoo*, is not dissimilar from the numerous whaling vessels that cruised the South
Pacific during the early nineteenth century. A bit more dilapidated it
may be, with its rotting bulwarks and tottering masts, but still much
the same, down to the "old horse-shoe nailed as a charm to the foremast" (*O* 46). Besides providing good luck (motif D1561.1.3), the nautical horseshoe, as one nineteenth-century observer claimed, also kept
"Witches and Wizards from hindering the voyage, or damaging the
ship" (motif G272.11).[1] Elsewhere, Melville wrote that pirates kept
horseshoes nailed to the masts of their vessels. In "A Thought on
Book-Binding," his review of James Fenimore Cooper's *Red Rover,*
he stated, "In the mysterious cyphers in bookbinders' relievo stamped
upon the covers we joyfully recognize a poetical signification and
pictorial shadowing forth of the horse-shoe, which in all honest and
God-fearing piratical vessels is invariably found nailed to the mast"
(*PT* 237–38). Another contemporary observer asserted that "scarcely
a boat or vessel puts to sea without this talisman."[2] Legend has it that
Admiral Nelson had a horseshoe nailed to the mast of the *Victory* at
Trafalgar.[3] Sailors are proverbially superstitious, and Melville's are no
exception. The lucky horseshoe is the most obvious sailor superstition that he included in his writings, but his nautical works abound
with numerous others much less obvious.

The superstitions and folk beliefs Melville used to literary advantage can be divided into three basic groups. The horseshoe belongs
with the first group, superstitious precautions sailors took to protect
themselves from harm at sea. Some of these precautions, like nailing
a horseshoe to the foremast, stipulate behaviors to carry out, while
others name behaviors to avoid. The second group of sailor superstitions concerns signs and omens. The portent of some signs was obvious to all but the greenest sailors, while chance appearances of more

mysterious objects, creatures, or visions could be understood only by the more experienced. The most mysterious signs required someone with second sight to interpret them, such as Finnish sailors, Skyemen, or those from other isolated places in northern Europe. The third group of superstitions concerns direct actions the sailor took to change his personal fortune. Such superstitious behaviors generally required the Devil's help, seldom explicitly but often implicitly. In short, Group One superstitions prevented bad things from happening; Group Two superstitions foresaw what would happen; and Group Three superstitions made things happen.

JUST AS THE HORSESHOE protected a vessel from danger, personal charms protected individual sailors from harm. The amulets Melville described have powerful associations, despite the frequently skeptical attitude his narrators evince. Some of Melville's lucky charms allude to early Christian belief. In *White-Jacket,* Jack Chase suggests that a chunk of rock from St. Paul's cave in Malta is "good for a charm against shipwreck"—or so he had heard, for he admits that he had not tried it himself (*WJ* 271). Aboard the *Neversink* in *White-Jacket* are old weather-beaten sailors who "carry about their persons bits of 'Old Ironsides,' as Catholics do the wood of the true cross" (*WJ* 9). With the simile, Melville paralleled Christian belief with the folk beliefs of the superstitious sailor. Linking them, he questioned the value of Christian amulets for protecting their wearers and, implicitly, the value of Christianity as a means of salvation.

Among American sailors, as White Jacket suggests, "Old Ironsides," officially the USS *Constitution,* held special powers. The seasoned frigate, rebuilt and restored to service during the 1830s, remained the finest ship in the fleet; a chip of its wood symbolized its seaworthiness and therefore protected its bearer from harm at sea. As Melville wrote in *Billy Budd,* "Everything is for a term venerated in navies. Any tangible object associated with some striking incident of the service is converted into a monument" (*BB* 131). Since the *Constitution* had never been defeated, it had a reputation as a lucky ship and had seemingly supernatural powers to defy traditionally bad omens. Sailors normally dreaded sailing on a Friday; Melville called Friday the "Day of Ill Luck" (*Co* 258), and in *Clarel* Agath explains that his doomed ship left "From Egypt bound for Venice sailing— / On Friday—well might heart forebode!" (*Cl* 3.12.75–76). But "the keel of

Old Ironsides," a contemporary observed, "was laid on Friday; she was launched on Friday; went to sea on Friday; and fought her first battle on Friday."[4] Anyone who carried a chip of wood from "Old Ironsides," therefore, could share its supernatural power.

The ship also symbolized the power of American democracy, a power graphically represented by its new figurehead, an effigy of Andrew Jackson, complete with cloak, hat, stick, and a scroll representing the Constitution of the United States.[5] A vessel's figurehead held great symbolic power, and its disfigurement, as the events of "Benito Cereno" suggest, indicated ill fortune. Landsmen were not immune to the symbolic power of "Old Ironsides," as Melville stated elsewhere. Predicting in a letter to his brother Gansevoort that the Mexican War might provoke a major dispute that would dwarf all previous American conflicts, Melville hinted that such a war would diminish the frigate's supernatural power: "Lord, the day is at hand, when ... canes made out of the Constitution's timbers be thought no more of than bamboos" (*Co* 41).[6]

One of the most powerful personal charms was a caul, the fetal membrane that in some cases covered the face or head of a newborn infant. To carry a caul protected its bearer from drowning, and according to belief, no ship with one on board could sink. Being born with one not only protected a person from drowning but also gave him supernatural clairvoyance and allowed him to see supernatural sights, such as ghosts and spirits, hidden from ordinary eyes.[7] Describing "Mad Jack," White-Jacket imagines his birth: "For in some time of tempest—off Cape Horn or Hatteras—*Mad Jack* must have entered the world—such things have been—not with a silver spoon, but with a speaking-trumpet in his mouth; wrapped up in a caul, as in a main-sail—for a charmed life against shipwrecks he bears" (*WJ* 33).

In *Moby-Dick,* Ahab carries a small vial of sand filled with Nantucket soundings as a pocket charm, a fact not revealed until late in the book (*MD* 495). Ahab's amulet reflects traditional motifs—magic sand (D935.1), magic dirt as protection (D1380.9)—yet Ishmael's description of the vial's contents is detailed enough to elicit more specific associations. Earlier in his narrative Ishmael had described Nantucket as "a mere hillock, and elbow of sand; all beach, without a background. There is more sand there than you would use in twenty years as a substitute for blotting paper" (*MD* 63). His geologic description continues at some length, and with considerable humor. By giving Ahab sand from Nantucket soundings (that is, the sea floor) rather than from Nantucket itself, however, Melville detached Ahab from his home and his charm from any humorous associations.

Sand was sometimes used to guard against evil spirits.[8] In legend, sand serves to ward off the Devil, who is often given such impossible tasks as twisting ropes from sand or counting all the grains of sand on a beach before he can effect harm. Ahab's pocket amulet might require the Devil to count the grains of sand inside the vial before he could touch its bearer, but the fact that the sand specifically comes from soundings suggests a different interpretation. Among the sailor proverbs Melville recorded in *White-Jacket* is the "merchant seamen's maxim, that *there are no Sundays off soundings*" (*WJ* 155). The proverb, of course, meant that sailors nearing shore could not observe the Sabbath, for they had to work in order to navigate the ship safely. Using the amulet to link Ahab with soundings, Melville subtly recalled the proverb and thus reinforced Stubb's suggestion that Ahab did not observe the Sabbath: "I never yet saw him kneel" (*MD* 229). There are no Sundays for Ahab.

Lucky charms had one problem. In the sailor's rough-and-tumble, knockabout life there was always the chance that a pocket or a necklace charm could be lost or stolen. Happily, one type of charm was sure to stick with the sailor, even if he were stripped of all his material possessions: tattoos were permanent. Of course, not just any tattoo would work as a charm, and it could not be slapped just anywhere on the body. For greatest efficacy, the tattoo or tattoos had to be placed on the limbs.

The sailors aboard the *Neversink* are anxious to have crucifixes tattooed on themselves, for as White Jacket sardonically explains, "They affirm—some of them—that if you have that mark tattooed upon all four limbs, you might fall overboard among seven hundred and seventy-five thousand white sharks, all dinnerless, and not one of them would so much as dare to smell at your little finger" (*WJ* 171). Jarl, the superstitious Skyeman of *Mardi*, has such a tattoo, "a characteristic device upon the arm of the wonderful mariner—our Saviour on the cross, in blue; with the crown of thorns, and three drops of blood in vermilion, falling one by one from each hand and foot" (*M* 147). In *Clarel*, Agath is similarly adorned:

> Upon the fore-arm did appear
> A thing of art, vermil and blue,
> A crucifixion in tattoo,
> With trickling blood-drops strange to see.
> (*Cl* 4.2.49–52)

Clarel also contains a good description of how tattooing traditions were perpetuated among sailors. Agath explains:

> "We seamen, where there's naught to do
> In calms, the straw for hats we plait,
> Or one another we tattoo
> With marks we copy from a mate,
> Which he has from his elders ta'en,
> And those from prior ones again;
> And few, if any, think or reck
> But so with pains their skin to deck.
> This crucifixion, though, by some
> A charm is held 'gainst watery doom."
> (*Cl* 4.2.87-96)

Similarly, Daniel Orme has "a crucifix in indigo and vermilion tattooed on the chest and on the side of the heart."[9] Some contemporary sailors had crucifixes tattooed on their backs as a way to evoke sympathy from an officer in charge of flogging and thus lessen the punishment's severity.[10]

The crucifix was not the only tattooed icon that could protect a sailor from harm. According to tradition, a rooster tattooed on one foot and a pig on the other guarded against drowning.[11] These same icons would also protect a sailor from starving to death, for he always had his egg and bacon with him. The pig icon commonly protected sailors from harm. Some held that the pig should be tattooed on the knee instead of the ankle, a rhyming superstition difficult to forget:

> Pig on the knee
>
> Safety at sea.[12]

For whatever reason, the pig had particularly rich superstitious resonances among sailors, but not all brought good luck—quite the contrary. Pronouncing the word "pig" aboard ship was sure to bring forth bad luck; instead, sailors referred to the pig as "Mr. Dennis," "Little Fellah," or "Gruff." These swinish superstitions suggest a curious separation between image and name: as an icon, the pig was lucky; as a name, it was unlucky. Seeing a pig could also be unlucky for the sailor. Fishermen who saw a pig on the way to the waterfront would not fish that day.[13] Aboard the *Neversink,* White-Jacket hears a story of a battle at sea during which a pig, covered with the blood of fallen sailors, was tossed overboard by the conquerors, who believed it would be bad luck to eat it (*WJ* 316).

The taboo against pronouncing the word "pig" aboard ship is just one precautionary superstition of many stipulating behaviors the sailor should avoid. Like superstitious landlubbers, sailors tried to avoid anything associated with the number thirteen. Never sign aboard a vessel with thirteen letters in its name; never leave for a voyage on the thirteenth of the month;[14] and never have thirteen men in a mess. After White-Jacket is ousted by his original messmates, Jack Chase takes him into his mess, to the consternation of Chase's fellow messmates—White-Jacket makes thirteen. Once he joins their group, other members start dying. One of the survivors remarks, "This comes of having *thirteen* in the mess. . . . [B]last it, it warn't till White-Jacket there comed into the mess that these here things began" (*WJ* 332).

Never steer a ship using a compass with an inverted needle. Doing so, as Ahab knows, prompts "shudderings and evil portents" among the crew (*MD* 518). To avoid bad luck, according to another superstition, never place a black trunk aboard ship.[15] In *Moby-Dick* Melville did not expressly use this superstition, but at one point he compares the Negro Pip to "a hurried traveller's trunk" and thus obliquely alludes to it (*MD* 413). Never sail with brothers aboard ship.[16] In *The Sea Beast,* Warner Brothers' silent adaptation of *Moby-Dick,* Ahab, played by the great profile John Barrymore, loses his leg to the white whale while a harpooneer aboard a ship named *The Three Brothers.* In *Moby-Dick* the captain of the *Rachel* had left home with his two sons aboard, and the younger is lost at sea.

The name of a ship prompted many superstitious beliefs. No shipowner with an ear to sailor talk would name a ship *The Three Brothers,* for superstitious sailors would not sign aboard a vessel with that name. Never change a ship's name; doing so prefigures death.[17] Apparently unaware of the superstition, Israel Potter asks John Paul Jones to change the name of his ship. Jones tells him that changing the name would go against superstition, yet nevertheless agrees to Potter's suggested name, *Poor Richard,* which they frenchify to *Bon Homme Richard* (*IP* 115).

The sea was a fickle mistress, and the sailor should always avoid teasing her. Offer her a part of you, and she will take all. In *Mardi* Jarl and the narrator board a seemingly abandoned ship and discover two survivors, Samoa and his mate, Annatoo. Samoa's arm, badly wounded, must be amputated. After the amputation Samoa refuses to toss the limb overboard, being "superstitiously averse to burying in the sea the dead limb of a body yet living; since in that case Samoa held, that he must very soon drown and follow it" (*M* 78).

White-Jacket contains a similar superstition. Unable to auction off his loathsome grego, White-Jacket considers burying it at sea but stops short due to "certain involuntary superstitious considerations." The jacket, he thinks, "will be sure to spread itself into a bed at the bottom of the sea, upon which I shall sooner or later recline, a dead man" (*WJ* 203). Though White-Jacket generally raises a skeptical eyebrow at the numerous sailor superstitions he describes, this particular one is so powerful that he cannot help but surrender to it. In a way, the idea of White-Jacket submerging his characteristic garment at sea is an even more serious violation of the superstition than Samoa burying his amputated limb. In submerging the grego, White-Jacket would be not only relinquishing part of himself but giving up the thing that supplied his identity. No wonder he succumbs to the superstition.

White-Jacket's superstitious fear of letting his grego fall to the ocean floor anticipates a late episode in *Moby-Dick.* In Chapter 130, "The Hat," a black sea hawk, a bird Melville elsewhere calls a "fierce black bandit" (*PT* 414), swoops upon Ahab and snatches his hat. Ishmael finds a parallel between the episode and the Roman myth of an eagle seizing Tarquin's hat in prophecy that Tarquin would ascend to the throne of Rome. The parallel is not exact, as Ishmael realizes, for only when the eagle replaced the hat on Tarquin's head was the omen made good (*MD* 539). In *Moby-Dick* the hawk ascends to a great height and drops Ahab's hat, which falls into the sea. Never place your hat on the bed, goes a commonplace domestic superstition, for doing so would cause bad luck.[18] A hat that falls to the ocean bed would presumably bring similar bad luck. The fate of Ahab's hat foreshadows his own.

Sailor superstitions give the sea human qualities. She is jealous, grasping, vindictive, vengeful. These anthropomorphic associations affect other folk beliefs about the sea. Many concern drowning. Sailors often believed that people drowned because the sea took them of its own conscious will. Some never learned to swim, for they believed that once the sea took them, it was useless to fight back. Sailors who could swim sometimes did not rescue people from drowning, in fear that the vengeful sea, deprived of one victim, would claim another, specifically the rescuer.[19] When Queequeg saved the drowning man between New Bedford and Nantucket, he sealed his own fate.

NUMEROUS OTHER SUPERSTITIONS Melville used in his writings involve omens, chance sights and events that indicate the future to anyone who can recognize their meaning. Some events were so obvious that even the rankest greenhorn could not help but understand them. When a man commits suicide from the *Highlander,* Wellingborough Redburn guesses that the suicide prefigures an "ill-omened voyage" (*R* 51). Understanding the traditional meaning of other chance occurrences at sea, however, required more experience or, oftentimes, supernatural clairvoyance. In *Mardi* a shovel-nosed shark, well attended by pilot fish, begins following the small craft in which the two sailors have escaped. They kill the shark, which sinks from sight. Its accompanying pilot fish disappear along with it, but soon three pilot fish reappear and begin following the boat just as they had followed the shark: "A good omen," says Jarl, "no harm will befall us so long as they stay" (*M* 55).

Porpoises, too, sailors saw as good omens. Ishmael explains that the porpoise's "appearance is generally hailed with delight by the mariner. Full of fine spirits, they invariably come from the breezy billows to windward. They are the lads that always live before the wind. They are accounted a lucky omen" (*MD* 143).[20] The sight of the giant squid, on the other hand, to mention an ominous marine animal, is so rare that whalemen "invest it with portentousness" (*MD* 276). Starbuck says that few whale ships ever behold the great squid and return to their ports to tell of it. For Queequeg, on the other hand, locating a giant squid is a sign that a sperm whale will appear soon. This sea creature continues to hold great symbolic power; many people nowadays pay homage to the giant squid display whenever they visit the Smithsonian.

The round cork life buoy that the crew of the *Neversink* locates in *White-Jacket* represents an ineffectual attempt to rescue a sailor gone overboard, but the buoy itself is not necessarily ominous. The white bird that hovers over the buoy really provides the omen; for, according to sailor belief, white sea birds are the souls of departed sailors haunting the place where they died. Seeing a white bird accompanying the buoy, one officer cries out, "Bad luck! bad luck! . . . [W]e'll number one less before long" (*WJ* 71). Sure enough, the omen soon comes true: a crew member drowns shortly after. The belief that white sea birds were the souls of departed sailors was held the world over. Sometimes the soul became an albatross, or a "goney bird," but the soul could also become a sea gull or a stormy petrel, a type of bird more commonly known as the Mother Carey's chicken.[21]

References to white sea birds abound in Melville's writings. In *White-Jacket*, Jack Chase notices a white bird and points it out to the others. White-Jacket explains, "Gazing upward, all beheld a snow-white, solitary fowl, which—whence coming no one could tell—had been hovering over the main-mast during the service, and was now sailing far up into the depths of the sky" (*WJ* 342). In a footnote to "The Whiteness of the Whale," Ishmael describes the flight of an albatross Heavenward "to join the wing-folding, the invoking, and adoring cherubim!" (*MD* 190). In "The Encantadas," Melville called the albatross "the snow-white ghost of the haunted Capes of Hope and Horn" (*PT* 135). In his lecture "The South Seas," he mentioned "the storied albatross, with white and arching wing like an archangel's" (*PT* 414). As Billy Budd's corpse is committed to the sea, seafowl approach and circle the burial spot "with the moving shadow of their outstretched wings and the croaked requiem of their cries" (*BB* 127). Depending upon the context, the sight of these birds could either be a good or a bad omen, but one thing was beyond dispute: killing one meant bad luck.

The average sailor could learn to recognize and understand these traditional signs after only a voyage or two, but some sailors had the second sight, a supernatural gift for interpreting signs and making prophecies. Melville knew about the second sight from his sailor experiences, yet he also read about it.[22] Sailors traditionally attributed supernatural clairvoyance to Finns—a term applied not just to seamen from Finland but to anyone from Scandinavia or, even more generally, northern Europe. As Melville wrote in *Omoo,* Finnish sailors "are supposed to possess the gift of second sight" (*O* 46). In *Mardi* Melville's narrator finds an old oaken box covered with inscriptions and carvings, including "divers mystic diagrams in chalk, drawn by old Finnish mariners, in casting horoscopes and prophecies. Your old tars are all Daniels" (*M* 64). The last statement suggests that being a Finn was not essential for the mariner-prophet; old age seems a more fundamental characteristic. Nevertheless, sailors from isolated places in northern Europe had more prophetic abilities, according to tradition. Jarl hails from the Isle of Skye; aboard the *Pequod* is a Manxman, a native from the Isle of Man, who is "an old sepulchral man" and indeed the oldest man aboard. Ishmael explains that "the old sea-traditions, the immemorial credulities, popularly invested this old Manxman with preternatural powers of discernment" (*MD* 124).[23] The Manxman admits he had studied with an old witch in Copenhagen, an admission that conjures up images of the legendary Black School.

Early in *Moby-Dick* the Manxman discerns that Ahab has a birthmark reaching from crown to sole. Later he explains strange and disturbing sounds the crew hears one evening, cries "so plaintively wild and unearthly—like articulated wailings of the ghosts of all Herod's murdered Innocents." The moans are "the voices of newly drowned men in the sea." The fact that the sounds turn out to be seals' cries in no way minimizes their dark portent. Ishmael explains that "most mariners cherish a very superstitious feeling about seals, arising not only from their peculiar tones when in distress, but also from the human look of their round heads and semi-intelligent faces" (*MD* 523–24). Seals were often considered the souls of drowned sailors, and their moans prefigured further death.

THE THIRD GROUP OF SUPERSTITIONS required the sailor to take steps to change the future—his, his ship's, or his enemy's. In order to work these efforts needed supernatural assistance from the Prince of Darkness himself. In Melville's day, serious attempts at conjuring required the sailor to call on Satan's help explicitly, but the more commonplace superstitious practices had become detached from their satanic associations.

Some of the common shipboard superstitions concerned whistling. Generally it was considered bad luck to whistle on board ship, because it would bring forth strong winds and storms (motif D2142.1.6).[24] Wind was associated with the Devil (motif G303.6.3.3), and a gust of wind often anticipated the Devil's appearance (motif G303.6.3.5). A common proverbial comparison among sailors was to be "as busy as a devil in a gale of wind."[25] An eighteenth-century observer explained, "Our sailors, I am told, at this very day, I mean the vulgar sort of them, have a strange opinion of the devil's power and agency in stirring up winds, and that this is the reason why they so seldom whistle on ship-board, esteeming that to be a *mocking*, and consequently an enraging of the devil."[26]

Despite superstitions against whistling, sailors often whistled when they were becalmed.[27] As the *Highlander* approaches home in *Redburn* it is beset by a calm, whereupon the sailors "whistled and whistled for a wind" (*R* 298). Becalmed near Cape Horn in *White-Jacket,* the sailors aboard the *Neversink* can do little but whistle: "There was nothing to be done but patiently to await the pleasure of the elements, and 'whistle for a wind,' the usual practice of seamen in a calm" (*WJ* 101). Indeed, the practice had become so commonplace that the phrase, as Melville's inverted commas suggest, had become proverbial.[28] Though whistling for a wind was common, it was not without danger; sailors could get more wind than they bargained for, as happens to the *Neversink* as it approaches the Cape. The practice had become largely disassociated from Satan, but make no mistake, whistling for a wind, as at least one contemporary writer recognized, "was a direct invocation to 'the prince of the power of the air' to exert himself in their behalf."[29]

Other methods for raising a wind more clearly required satanic assistance. In *Redburn,* Jack Blunt, Melville's favorite superstitious sailor, has "some wild Irish words he used to mutter over during a calm for a fair wind" (*R* 88; motif D2141.0.7). As do other superstitious sailors, Blunt finds intimidating the behavior of Mrs. O'Brien, one of the numerous Irish emigrants aboard the *Highlander* on its return journey. Mrs. O'Brien has "a large old quarto Bible, black with age," which she reads aloud to her children. The sailors develop "a bitter grudge against her book. To that, and the incantations muttered over it, they ascribed the head winds that haunted us." Jack

Blunt "believed that Mrs. O'Brien purposely came on deck every morning, in order to secure a foul wind for the next ensuing twenty-four hours" (*R* 268). Believing that incantations can be used to raise a wind, Blunt can assign no other purpose to Mrs. O'Brien's activities. Incantations were threatening enough in themselves, but in the sailors' eyes Mrs. O'Brien makes them even more intimidating by using a book. The fact that hers is a black book further enhances its supernatural power.[30] No matter that it was the Holy Scriptures or that she was merely conducting her family's devotions—anyone in contact with the spirit world for devout purposes could just as easily use spirits for evil ones. For that reason clergymen were unwelcome on a ship. According to superstition, the clergyman, known by the derisive epithet "Foul-weather Jack," brought inclement weather.[31]

Unsurprisingly, Finns and Manxmen also had supernatural power over natural forces. Numerous northern European legends tell how local wizards controlled the winds. In *Two Years Before the Mast* Richard Henry Dana wrote that the ship's cook believed Finns to be wizards with "power over winds and storms." Another sailor aboard Dana's vessel concurs, recalling an episode when a Finn conjured up a head wind after the captain had spoken harshly to him.[32] Echoing Dana, Melville wrote that the Finns had "the power to wreak supernatural vengeance upon those who offend them" (*O* 46). As soon as John Paul Jones has sailed the *Ranger* past the Isle of Man in *Israel Potter,* the wind shifts and blows with renewed vigor (*IP* 96).

Though he often took a skeptical tone as he described the sailor superstitions, Melville could not mask his fascination with these beliefs and practices. His numerous, colorful references throughout his writings to sailor superstitions do much to recapture the atmosphere of the sailing ship. Often, however, they do much more. By the time he came to *Moby-Dick,* as subsequent chapters will show, he realized that carefully placed superstitions could draw readers into the sailor's world in a way that could change them forever.

· T W O ·

Fiction and
Folksong

Few aspects of native culture escape Tommo's scrutiny in *Typee*, and traditional music is no exception. Partway through the story, he describes one of the Typee's raucous vocal performances and his own subsequent efforts to amuse King Mehevi and his entourage with a stanza from "The Bavarian Broomseller." Melville did not quote the traditional song, but it begins something like this:

> From Deutchland I come with my light wares all laden,
> To the land where the blessing of freedom doth bloom.
> Then listen, fair lady and young pretty maiden,
> Oh, buy of the wandering Bavarian a broom.[1]

The stanza amazes Mehevi and the others. It is as if Tommo has "some preternatural faculty which Heaven had denied to them" (*T* 227). Try as they might, Mehevi and company cannot sing the song themselves, so they settle for listening to Tommo repeat it countless times. The incident greatly enhances Tommo's reputation among the Typees. Afterward they often call upon him to regale them with song, and he takes on the nominal role of court minstrel.

Though it is always risky to equate Tommo's actions with Melville's, it is not hard to imagine Melville himself singing songs during his Marquesan sojourn. On his earliest sailor voyage aboard the *St. Lawrence* (the model for the *Highlander* in *Redburn)* and on the *Acushnet* prior to his desertion in Nukuheva, he had ample opportunity to learn ballads, sea shanties, and whaling songs. Shanties, after all, were working songs essential for carrying out his nautical duties. Shipmate Richard Tobias Greene later reminisced in a letter to Melville, "My mind often reverts to the many pleasant moonlight watches we passed together on the deck of the 'Acushnet' as we whiled away the hours with yarn and song till 'eight bells'" (*Co* 685–86).

Melville's numerous allusions to folksongs throughout his fiction attest to his interest in traditional music. If he had indeed sung well-remembered songs in the Marquesas, it seems likely that he sang others in addition to "The Bavarian Broomseller." The reference to this particular song in *Typee,* therefore, deserves further consideration.

The broomseller sings of wandering westward from his native homeland to England, where he had begun selling brooms as a London street crier. In the second stanza of one recorded version, the singer attempts to persuade potential buyers to purchase a broom to "brush away insects that sometimes annoy you" and to "sweep all vexatious intruders away." The third stanza takes a different approach, appealing to the buyer's sense of urgency as he explains that he will be leaving England soon to return home. He also appeals to the buyer's sentiment and expresses his fondness for England and gratitude to those who purchase his wares. In rough outline, the situation of the Bavarian broomseller is not dissimilar from that of Tommo in *Typee.* Tommo has traveled westward to a foreign land too. Though he shoulders no sack of brooms, he does bear his cultural baggage, which he disseminates among the natives. He introduces the Typees to needle and thread and makes pop-guns for them. Ultimately he, too, longs to leave the foreign land and return home, but like the broomseller, he also is trapped. The broomseller cannot return home until he sells enough brooms to pay passage back. The English householders must accept and purchase what he has to offer before he may leave. Tommo's plight is more complex. Though the Typees partially accept his Western culture, they ultimately try to acculturate *him* with a facial tattoo, a mark which would effectively prevent him from ever returning to his own land. As the song ends, the broomseller remains in a foreign land, longing for home. As Tommo finishes singing it, he is no closer to home either; rather, he has been further assimilated into Mehevi's world, in his new role as minstrel.

"The Bavarian Broomseller" looks forward to much of Melville's later fiction. It tells a basic story that would long fascinate him, the story of the *isolato,* a person lost and alone, stranded on an island. The broomseller's plight most closely parallels that of Israel Potter, who also finds himself stranded in England, unable to afford passage home, working as a street crier to sell his wares. Melville treated similar subjects in other fiction, most notably the later sketches of "The Encantadas."

Melville's use of "The Bavarian Broomseller" in *Typee* also anticipates his use of folksongs in his subsequent fiction. In his novels, short stories, and sketches he often alluded to traditional songs, sometimes quoting a few lines from them, and quickly resuming the narrative. For readers familiar with the songs, the allusions, brief as they are, supply a counterpoint to his fictional narrative. The folksong allowed Melville to give verse echoes to his prose text. In so doing, he allowed another voice to speak without relinquishing narrative control. During the course of his writing career, Melville's use of folksongs becomes subtler. In later works, he would mention folksinging yet name no particular song. He used the mere sound of singing, combined with keen visual description, to create striking composites of prose, music, and visual imagery.

FOLKSONG REFERENCES ARE plentiful in *Omoo*—the *Julia*'s crew sings windlass songs, Dr. Long Ghost sings "an old hunting-song—Tallyho," drunken revellers sing "Sailing down, sailing down, / On the coast of *Barbaree*" (*O* 149, 223, 292)—but the book which followed *Omoo* contains few allusions to traditional song. As the narrator tells his readers in the early pages of *Mardi*, he had tired of hearing sea shanties and found that the "everlasting stanzas of Black-eyed Susan sung by our forecastle choir" were "Staler than stale ale" and that "Ned Ballad's songs were sung till the echoes lurked in the very tops, and nested in the bunts of the sails" (*M* 5). Melville does include a ballad singer named Yoomy among *Mardi*'s cast of characters, but Yoomy's songs owe little to traditional music; rather, he is an allegorical standin. Seeking to lampoon contemporary written culture, Melville imagines an allegorical oral culture. Yoomy more accurately represents contemporary American poetasters than traditional ballad singers. Melville's greater purpose in *Mardi*, of course, concerns the quest for truth, which has its own allegorical stand-in, Yillah. In a way, the narrator's rejection of ballads and sailor songs is ironic, for they remain important to the plot, such as it is. The song the narrator so tires of hearing, "Black-Eyed Susan," describes a character fundamentally opposite to Yillah and thus supplies a poignant contrast.

"Black-Eyed Susan" tells the story of a sailor's sweetheart who waits patiently and faithfully for him to come home from the sea, while he, just as faithful and patient, never seeks another throughout his peregrinations. The sailor, William by name, tells her:

If to fair India's coast we sail
Thine eyes are seen in diamonds bright,
Thy breath is Afric's spicy gale,
Thy teeth as ivory so bright,
And every beauteous object that I view
Wakes in my soul, wakes in my soul
Sweet vision bright of you.[2]

Susan represents the safety and sanctity of home and hearth. When William ultimately returns home he knows exactly where he can find his dark-eyed beauty, and he also knows that her devotion to him will not have wavered. Yillah, in contrast, has "blue, firmament eyes" (*M* 136). Rescued from her captivity, she eludes her rescuers and disappears from sight. The sailor-narrator must search for her, but he has no idea where she is, what she is doing, or whether she even remembers him. He has no guarantee that the long and arduous search will succeed, that he will ever find blue-eyed Yillah.

MARDI FAILED COMMERCIALLY, and it also fails aesthetically, in part because Melville assumed the persona of a philosopher-aesthete at the cost of his sailor voice. With his next two books, Melville would recapture the sailor's voice and produce two more approachable, if less ambitious, works. On one hand, it is disappointing to see Melville revert to narratives based on personal experience after his unsuccessful attempt to reach new literary heights in *Mardi*. Melville himself saw *Redburn* and *White-Jacket* as two works well below his ability, works written to atone for *Mardi*'s extravagance and to show his family he could be a good provider.[3] Though a retrograde movement, Melville's return to personal narrative after *Mardi* allowed him to give his prose greater texture. With references to folksongs in both *Redburn* and *White-Jacket,* Melville reaffirmed the voice of the simple sailor. When he came to *Moby-Dick* he was able to accomplish what he had not in *Mardi:* to blend his metaphysical speculations with the sailor's voice. Banished in *Mardi*, Ned Ballad returns with a vengeance in *Redburn, White-Jacket,* and *Moby-Dick.*

In *Redburn* Melville emphasized the value of song for accomplishing work among sailors, something which he had recognized previously in *Omoo:* "Where the work to be accomplished is any way difficult, this mode of enlivening toil is quite efficacious among sailors. So, willing to make every thing as cheerful as possible, Shorty struck up, 'Were you ever in Dumbarton?' a marvelously inspiring, but somewhat indecorous windlass chorus" (*O* 206). Melville did not quote the song, but it goes something like this:

> Were you ever in Dumbarton,
> Where they wear the tartan,
> Where they wear the tartan,
> Little above the knee?
> My love she is so neat and small,
> She won't have me at all,
> But try to get her full
> And then she'll marry me.[4]

Wellingborough Redburn's detailed description conveys the mood of shanty singing aboard a merchant ship:

The men took hold of the rope, and began pulling upon it; the foremost man of all setting up a song with no words to it, only a strange musical rise and fall of notes. In the dark night, and far out upon the lonely sea, it sounded wild enough, and made me feel as I had sometimes felt, when a twilight room a cousin of mine, with black eyes, used to play some old German airs on the piano. I almost looked round for goblins, and felt just a little bit afraid. But I soon got used to this singing; for the sailors never touched a rope without it. Sometimes, when no one happened to strike up, and the pulling, whatever it might be, did not seem to be getting forward very well, the mate would always say, *"Come, men, can't any of you sing? Sing now, and raise the dead."* And then some one of them would begin, and if every man's arms were as much relieved as mine by the song, and he could pull as much better as I did, with such a cheering accompaniment, I am sure the song was well worth the breath expended on it. It is a great thing in a sailor to know how to sing well, for he gets a great name by it from the officers, and a good deal of popularity among his shipmates. Some sea-captains, before shipping a man, always ask him whether he can sing out at a rope. (*R* 45–46)

White-Jacket, too, mentions the usefulness of song for accomplishing work but is disappointed that sea shanties are strictly forbidden in the navy. As a result, only the three black cooks aboard the

Neversink—Sunshine, Rosewater, and May-day—can enjoy song while they work. Sunshine, White-Jacket explains, often regales his fellow cooks "with some remarkable St. Domingo melodies." Melville then quoted the following lines:

> Oh! I los' my shoe in an old canoe,
> Johnio! come Winum so!
> Oh! I los' my boot in a pilot-boat,
> Johnio! come Winum so!
> Den rub-a-dub de copper, oh!
> Oh! copper rub-a-dub-a-oh! (*WJ* 58)

White-Jacket also encounters Negro folksongs, through his chance reading. In "A Man-of-War Library," he specifically mentions "a Negro Song-book, containing *Sittin' on a Rail, Gumbo Squash,* and *Jim along Josey*" (*WJ* 168–69). Melville borrowed the reference to these Negro songs from one of his key sources for *White-Jacket, Life in a Man-of-War; or Scenes in "Old Ironsides" during Her Cruise in the Pacific;*[5] he may have known published collections of songs such as the important compilation, *Negro Singers Own Song Book* (Philadelphia, [1843?]).

White-Jacket borrows the Negro songbook from one of his fellow sailors. From Rosewater, on the other hand, he obtains Thomas Moore's *Loves of the Angels.* Lending White-Jacket his copy of Moore, Rosewater maligns the Negro songbook as "vulgar stuff" and asserts the superiority of the polite writers. The contrast Melville establishes between the attitudes of white sailor and black cook is ironic. The publication of such works as the *Negro Singers Own Song Book* indicates the established culture's recognition of Negro folksongs as a vital form of expression. The black cook's rejection of the African-American tradition in favor of English belles lettres shows him discarding his folk heritage in an effort to assimilate himself within the established culture.

For White-Jacket, no one better represented the proper balance between high culture and folk culture than Jack Chase. He can recite Homer, Chaucer, and Camoens, but he also can sing centuries-old traditional "salt-sea ballads." "The Mermaid" tells a story of a shipwreck and incorporates a superstition about sailing on Friday. Many versions have been recorded. One begins:

One Friday morn when we set sail,
Not very far from land,
We there did espy a fair pretty maid
With a comb and a glass in her hand, her hand, her hand
With a comb and a glass in her hand.
While the raging seas did roar,
And the stormy winds did blow,
While we jolly sailor-boys were up into the top,
And the land-lubbers lying down below, below, below,
And the land-lubbers lying down below.[6]

Jack Chase also sings "Sir Patrick Spens," another centuries-old traditional ballad, which has been recorded in numerous variants. Most begin something like:

The king sat in Dumfermline toun,
Drinking the blude red wine:
"Where will I get a bold sailor,
To sail this ship o mine?"

Out then spak an auld auld knicht,
Was nigh the king akin:
"Sir Patrick Spens is the best sailor
That ever sailed the main."[7]

Jack Chase also knows "Spanish Ladies," a long-popular sailor song which White-Jacket calls "a favorite thing with British man-of-war's men" and which the crew of the *Pequod* sings in *Moby-Dick*.[8] It begins:

Fare ye well and adieu to the old Spanish ladies!
Fare ye well and adieu to the ladies of Spain!
For we have received orders to sail for old England,
And I hope in a short time to see you again.[9]

Hershel Parker reminds us of the importance of the *United States,* the real-life model for White-Jacket's *Neversink,* to the development of Melville's intellectual and belletristic interests; Jack Chase aboard the *Neversink* probably differs little from the real-life Jack Chase aboard the *United States*.[10] Chase gave Melville his first survey course in world literature, a survey that celebrated ancient, medieval, and Renaissance literary verse without ignoring songs from the oral tradition.

In *MOBY-DICK*, Melville, in turn, paid homage to both the literary classic and the folksong. Most of the extracts which preface the book come from written sources. Represented are important writers throughout the history of European literature: Bacon, Montaigne, Milton, Pope, Rabelais, Shakespeare. The final two extracts, however, are lines from traditional whaling songs. The next-to-last one is attributed simply to a "Nantucket Song":

> So be cheery, my lads, let your hearts never fail,
> While the bold harpooneer is striking the whale!
> (*MD* xxviii)

Linking a work of oral literature with the literary classics, Melville stressed the importance of the sailor's voice, an importance reinforced by the repetition of these same lines amidst the cacophony of sailor voices in Chapter 40, "Midnight, Forecastle."

Like nearly every facet of Melville's writing, his use of folksongs reached a new level of sophistication with *Moby-Dick*. Besides whaling songs, Melville also made use of sea shanties. In fact, he again used "Cheerly, Man," a halyard shanty he had mentioned before in *Omoo* and *Redburn*. The separate instances of one song's use over three books helps show how Melville's literary use of folksongs developed. "Cheerly, Man" had a solo part and a chorus. The soloist sang the first line, which would provide the name of a woman followed by a "Hi-oh!" or some variant; the chorus would respond with "Cheerly, Man!" In the next two solo lines the singer would describe the woman's behavior or appearance, each line rhyming, or at least coming close to rhyming, with the woman's last name. The final solo line would contain a direction for whatever nautical task was at hand, hauling at a line, for example. Sailors would pull at the final "oh!" of each solo line and the word "man!" in the chorus.

> Oh, Nancy Dawson, Hi-oh!
> *Cheerly, man!*
> She's got a notion, Hi-oh!

> *Cheerly man!*
>   For our old bo'sun, Hi-oh!
> *Cheerly, man!*
>   O! Haul-ee, Hi-oh!
> *Cheerly, man!*

Other recorded stanzas tell of Betsy Baker, who lived in Long Acre and married a Quaker; Polly Hawkins, with her white stockings, who beat all at talking; Kitty Karson, who jilted the parson to marry a mason; and Sally Racket, who pawned her man's jacket and then sold the ticket; among others. It is not hard to imagine that the structure combined with particularly rhythmic female names could make the song quite filthy. One prudish twentieth-century editor of American sailor songs apologized for presenting a greatly abbreviated text of "Cheerly, Man!": "The words are too racy to reproduce without considerable editing."[11]

The song was most used for tasks that required a coordinated hauling effort by many crew members, tasks such as catting the anchor and setting topsails.[12] Since these tasks helped bring a ship from port and get it under way, the sound of "Cheerly, Man!" was the sound of going home. When in *Omoo* it becomes clear that the men confined to the calabooza have no intention of returning to the *Julia*, the ship sails. Left behind, they watch and listen to the vessel depart: "The decks were all life and commotion; the sailors on the forecastle singing 'Ho, cheerly men!' as they catted the anchor" (*O* 149). The ship sails from sight, never to be seen again by the stranded prisoners. They are close enough to the water to hear their replacements aboard the *Julia* singing, but they themselves can neither sing the song nor get any closer to home. The normally happy song takes on an air of sadness as the ship fades from sight and the song from earshot. The image of the departing ship combined with the shanty's sound create a feeling of melancholy, a feeling which the old lawyer from "Bartleby" might call "a not-unpleasing sadness."

In *Redburn*, the scene is reversed, for Wellingborough Redburn's ship, the *Highlander*, after an over-lengthy stay at Liverpool, is ready to depart. The day is ideal for sailing, and many vessels prepare to depart. Melville again combines visual imagery with sound: "The white sails glistened in the clear morning air like a great Eastern encampment of sultans; and from many a forecastle, came the deep mellow old song *Ho-o-he-yo, cheerily men!* as the crews catted their anchors" (*R* 240). Hearing others sing the song and being able to sing it themselves, Redburn and his fellow sailors share the excitement and anticipation of going home.

The sailors aboard the *Pequod* also know "Cheerly, Man," but their rendition of it has an effect considerably different from melancholy or joy. Late in the narrative, the *Pequod* is caught in a typhoon and appears doomed, but surprisingly the ill winds abate, and a fair breeze arrives. The blustery weather had foretold their destruction, but the pleasant change seemingly negates the bad omens. Ishmael explains, "Instantly the yards were squared, to the lively song of '*Ho! the fair wind! oh-he-yo, cheerly, men!*' the crew singing for joy, that so promising an event should so soon have falsified the evil portents preceding it" (*MD* 514). The threatening wind, however, was only one of many evil portents revealed to the *Pequod*'s crew before the final chase. The fair wind may have seemed a good omen, but it could not counteract the bad ones. The normally happy "Cheerly, Man!" thus takes on a dark quality in *Moby-Dick*. The change of winds from foul to fair gives the sailors hope that they will reach home before long, but their hope is in vain. The song they sing to raise the sails will more likely raise the devil. Instead of home, "Cheerly, Man" will lead the *Pequod* to its final resting place.

"Norfolk Isle and the Chola Widow," the eighth sketch of "The Encantadas," may represent Melville's finest use of folksong in his fiction, yet it is also his subtlest. The sketch begins as a sailing vessel prepares to depart from Norfolk Isle after two days of tortoise hunting. The narrator heaves at the windlass with another sailor. As he begins his story, however, the narrator does not mention that they were singing a windlass chorus as they did their work; that fact comes out later. His partner sees something moving inland and directs the narrator's attention to it. The narrator exclaims, "It's a bird; a white-winged bird; perhaps a—no; it is—it is a handkerchief" (*PT* 152). First perceiving the fluttering white object as a bird, he is on the verge of calling it an albatross, but he checks himself as he realizes that what he sees is not a dead soul but a live one, waving a kerchief.

The captain orders the vessel stopped and a boat dispatched to rescue the islander, who turns out to be Hunilla, a Chola woman widowed there. Her story, told at two removes, occupies much of the remaining sketch. Safely aboard the ship, she tells it in Spanish to the captain, who immediately translates her words to the anxious crew huddled around them listening eagerly. The narrator, a refined litterateur with a voice scarcely distinguishable from Melville's own, carefully reshapes her story. As he tells it, sailor songs figure prominently on three separate occasions.

Hunilla had come to Norfolk Isle with her husband and her brother to hunt tortoises for their valuable oil. They had engaged a French whaler to take them there and retrieve them four months later. After depositing them on the island, the French sailors had departed, singing; "the gazing three on shore answered the loud glee of the singing crew; and ere evening, the French craft was hull down in the distant sea, its masts three faintest lines which quickly faded from Hunilla's eye" (*PT* 153). In terms of perspective, the scene is reminiscent of the *Julia's* departure from Tahiti in *Omoo,* but here the departure of the French ship is not melancholy. Hunilla and the two men had had every reason to expect the vessel back at the appointed time. The French song has a celebratory quality as the sailors anticipate a profitable voyage trying out whales, while the islanders look forward to a profitable sojourn trying out tortoises.

After several weeks on the island, Hunilla's husband and her brother had fashioned a crude catamaran from local materials for an offshore fishing trip. Hunilla had watched them from shore:

> By some bad tide or hap, or natural negligence of joyfulness (for though they could not be heard, yet by their gestures they seemed singing at the time), forced in deep water against that iron bar, the ill-made catamaran was overset, and came all to pieces; when, dashed by broad-chested swells between their broken logs and the sharp teeth of the reef, both adventurers perished before Hunilla's eyes. (*PT* 154)

Though the two men had been out of earshot, Hunilla knew them well enough that she could tell by sight that they had been singing. In their song's silence, however, it changed from sea shanty to funeral dirge.

Widowed and alone, Hunilla had waited in vain for the return of the French whaler. Other vessels had passed in the following months and years, but none rescued her. She had perceived the narrator's ship only by intuition, "by this isle's enchanted air." Living on the opposite side of the island from where the narrator and his fellow sailors had landed, she had traveled over the rugged inland terrain with the hope of signaling them before they departed from sight: "For when in crossing the isle Hunilla gained the high land in the centre, she must then for the first have perceived our masts, and also marked that their sails were being loosed, perhaps even heard the echoing chorus of the windlass song" (*PT* 158).

With the passage, the widow's story and the narrator's converge, but here the narrator reveals what he had not when he had begun his own story: that he and the other sailors were singing as they began to sail away. Paralleling the French whaler's departure, the incident emphasizes the trials Hunilla had undergone during the interim. Not only had she lost the two people she most loved, but also she had experienced nearly unendurable hardship, anguish, and loneliness. As the narrator retells her story, the melancholy sound of the slowly fading shanty underscores her forlornness.

As she had told her story, however, Hunilla had never said that she had heard them singing, a fact indicated by the narrator's "perhaps." The song is the narrator's deliberate artistic flourish. After the joyous singing of the French whalemen and the silent song anticipating death, the narrator finds it appropriate to add his own song to her story. What were they singing? Was it Shorty's indecorous "Were you ever in Dumbarton?" Or perhaps a song about the "girls in Booble Alley," which the hands at the *Pequod*'s windlass had sung with such unwitting good will before their voyage? He does not say, with good reason. Since the lyrics to windlass songs were often bawdy, a reference to a specific song would have detracted from the effect. Heard from a distance, the song evokes a somber mood that its off-color lyrics, heard nearby, could not.

Early in the sketch, the narrator describes his deliberate efforts to achieve artistic effect: "I wish I could but draw in crayons; for this woman was a most touching sight; and crayons, tracing softly melancholy lines, would best depict the mournful image of the dark-damasked Chola widow" (*PT* 152). Herman Melville accomplished with the written word what his narrator longs to do in crayon. The slight hint of song combined with a description of a vessel the moment its billowing sails begin to take it away from the island, its onlooker, a lonely, stranded widow desperately waving a white handkerchief, gives his prose sketch soft, blurry lines which have seldom been equaled in any artistic medium.

THREE

Proverb and
Irony

O n September 26, 1840, the mammoth weekly *Brother Jonathan* contained a humorous article lampooning various proverbs. Herman Melville's brother Gansevoort, then living in New York City, read the article and made note of it in his *Index Rerum:* "Proverbs: several of the most popular proverbs 'A bird in the hand &c' 'Like father like son' & many others ingeniously carped at." Around the time this issue of *Brother Jonathan* appeared, Herman returned to New York City from his westward travels. The article would have appealed to him. Already he had expressed his interest in vernacular speech, having mentioned "Bee's Slang Dictionary" in a letter to the *Albany Microscope* two years earlier (*Co* 14). The trip west would have furthered Herman's interest in slang, for Westerners already had a reputation for picturesque sayings, as Gansevoort had noted in his *Index Rerum* the week before, citing another article from *Brother Jonathan:* "Abbreviations: for an amusing & extensive collection of the slang abbreviations in use during the fever of speculation in '36 & '37 at the West see 'The Young Speculator: A Western Tale.'"[1]

In his correspondence, Melville often quoted proverbs. The classic letter he wrote his sister Kate in 1845, for instance, contains three in one sentence. After asserting that women named Kate were generally handsome, he wrote, "But, 'Fine feathers dont' make fine birds' & 'Handsome is, that handsome does' & all that sort of thing;—& so if the Kates were only distinguishable by their beautiful plumage, why, I would not give a fig for a Kate" (*Co* 28). The first two proverbs Melville separates from words of his own composition with inverted commas, indicating their status as traditional sayings. The third—not a full-fledged proverb but a proverbial phrase, "to give a fig"—contains the verb and object of the sentence's final independent clause. Family friend Sarah Morewood sent Melville an elaborately bound gilt copy of Edward Bulwer-Lytton's *Pilgrims of the Rhine;* Melville wrote her a letter of thanks paraphrasing the proverb, "Don't judge a book by its cover": "A superstitious, a fanciful mind might almost, by anticipation, distrust the wisdom taught by a book so bound" (*Co* 258).

In his published writings, Melville often used proverbs in much the same way he used them in his correspondence. Sometimes he elaborately paraphrased them, while at other times he deliberately called attention to their status as proverbs. Yet again he would integrate them within his text, so naturally that they must have been part of his everyday speech. The proverbial phrase about not giving a fig, for example, frequently recurs in his writing. In *Omoo* the narrator describes coming under the scrutiny of a missionary's wife, asserting that her old-fashioned cap "seemed to convey a prim rebuke"; he expresses his discomfort by stating, "As for the mob cap, not a fig did I care for it" (*O* 167). Contemplating Captain Riga's unkempt appearance in the presence of a young woman, Wellingborough Redburn imagines the captain must have been the woman's guardian, "for many guardians do not care one fig how shabby they look" (*R* 110). The practical-minded wife in "I and My Chimney" "cares not a fig" for her husband's "philosophical jabber" (*PT* 376). Also, the late poem "The Good Craft 'Snow-Bird'" depicts a ship transporting figs from a warmer clime to wintry Boston. In the final stanza, the speaker of the poem cheers on the vessel: "Bravo, master! Brava, brig! / For slanting snows out of the West / Never the *Snow-Bird* cares one fig" (*CP* 199). Seeing how often the phrase occurs in his written works, one can easily imagine Melville using it in conversation.

Yet Melville did much more with proverbs than merely include in his written work those which were part of his personal vocabulary. The first two proverbs he used in the sentence from the letter to Kate concern the disparity between appearance and reality, between seeming and being. Both are inherently ironic. A fine-looking bird, ironically, may not be a fine bird. As the Missouri bachelor says about the colorfully-attired cosmopolitan in *The Confidence-Man*, "Toucan fowl. Fine feathers on foul meat" (*CM* 131). Melville's writings contain many ironic proverbs. Those without their own built-in irony he often used in contexts that made them ironic. The *Snow-Bird,* after all, is a fig-carrying ship that cares not a fig. This late poem is light and playful, but Melville's proverbial irony sometimes takes on a darker hue.

Irony, of course, was not the only literary end to which Melville used proverbs. They serve many other purposes throughout his writings. His general fondness for proverbs often made them irresistible. Erasmus called proverbs *condimenta,* a characterization Melville would have esteemed, for he too saw them as a way to flavor his writings.[2] In one of the Burgundy Club sketches, the narrator describes the genial humor of Jack Gentian's club chitchat, finding it garnished "with sprigs of classic parsley set about it or inserted cloves of old English proverbs, or yet older Latin ones equally commonplace, yet never losing the verity in them, their preservative spice."[3] For Tommo in *Typee,* proverbs supply the wisdom he uses to cope with the unique situations he must face. In *Omoo* and *Mardi,* as Melville better understood his writer's craft he experimented by deliberately paraphrasing proverbs, using highfalutin' diction and intricate syntax for humorous effect. *Redburn* and *White-Jacket,* on the other hand, clearly show Melville taking great delight in recording quaint sailor sayings. His use of proverbs in these two works, therefore, parallels his use of sea shanties. Quoting both song and saying, Melville asserted the value of the sailor's voice. Still, irony more than any other common factor links together Melville's proverbs.

No proverb expresses the idea of irony more straightforwardly than "appearances are deceiving." Or, as the man with the wooden leg says in *The Confidence-Man,* "Looks are one thing, and facts are another"—a proverb that could serve as a motto for that book (*CM* 14). Melville had put this proverb to use well before *The Confidence-Man;* however, with some modification, it occurs in *Typee.* Discussing the Typees' religious iconography, Tommo mentions a local priest who bears a stubby wooden idol that seems to him "a mere pigmy in tatters." Realizing that it is a powerful object of worship, Tommo responds with a proverb: "But appearances all the world over are deceptive" (*T* 175). Tommo's departure from the proverb's simplest form shows him using his traditional knowledge to interpret a new situation and then incorporating what he has learned into his knowledge base. After his personal experience in the Antipodes, he can say that "appearances *all the world over* are deceptive."

Other proverbs Tommo mentions also show him using traditional wisdom to confront new situations. Early in the narrative, he describes eating the rain- and sweat-soaked, tobacco-flecked morsel of congealed hardtack crumbs; he declares, "What a true saying it is that 'appetite furnishes the best sauce'" (*T* 47). His new experience confirms the wisdom of the traditional saying. Much later in the narrative, after mentioning the seemingly distasteful native custom of eating raw fish, Tommo states, "When at Rome do as the Romans do, I hold to be so good a proverb, that being in Typee I made a point of doing as the Typees did" (*T* 209). He accepts their behavior to such an extent that he begins enjoying raw fish. Proverbial wisdom gives Tommo the capacity to face the unusual and survive.

Though his store of traditional wisdom serves Tommo well, it has limitations. When he approaches an aspect of native culture which he does not understand, he interprets it through his ethnocentric and egocentric point of view, without opening his mind to broader interpretations. Given the chance to learn more about native religion from Kory-Kory, for example, Tommo cannot learn as much as he had hoped, because as he himself confesses, he has not mastered the language. When Kory-Kory speaks of the afterlife, according to Tommo, he intimates that he is in no particular hurry to surrender this world for the next. Tommo's subsequent explanation virtually amounts to a definition of a proverb:

> Thus far, I think, I clearly comprehended Kory-Kory. But there was a singular expression he made use of at the time, enforced by as singular a gesture, the meaning of which I would have given much to penetrate. I am inclined to believe it must have been a proverb he uttered; for I afterwards heard him repeat the same words several times, and in what appeared to me to be a somewhat similar sense. Indeed, Kory-Kory had a great variety of short, smart-sounding sentences, with which he frequently enlivened his discourse; and he introduced them with an air which plainly intimated, that, in his opinion, they settled the matter in question, whatever it might be. (*T* 173)

Tommo plausibly conjectures that the Typee language contains proverbs, yet the proverb he attributes to Kory-Kory seems somewhat arbitrary: "Could it have been then, that when I asked him whether he desired to go to this heaven of bread-fruit, cocoa-nuts, and young ladies, which he had been describing, he answered by saying something equivalent to our old adage—'A bird in the hand is worth two in the bush'?—if he did, Kory-Kory was a discreet and sensible fellow, and I cannot sufficiently admire his shrewdness" (*T* 173).

The proverb was among the well-known ones which *Brother Jonathan* had "ingeniously carped at." While it had been used to juxtapose the here and the hereafter before—Emerson had written, "A world in the hand is worth two in the bush"—Tommo has no proof that Kory-Kory's verbal response was this proverb or any other.[4] Placing it in his mouth, Tommo projects his own personal attitude onto Kory-Kory. Hoping to confirm his own opinion toward the afterlife, Tommo hears what he wants to hear from Kory-Kory's speech, the true meaning of which, he had already confessed, he did not understand.

As Tommo's experiences in Typee show, visiting distant lands gave travellers the opportunity to put their traditional wisdom to the test. Melville himself said as much in his lecture on traveling. To use an example from the lecture, those who believed the proverbial comparison "cruel as a Turk" need only travel to Turkey and meet its people to disprove the proverb (*PT* 422). (In *Clarel* Melville would repeat and again refute the proverb [*Cl* 4.9.111]). Tommo's stay in Typee, however, does little to alter his proverbial wisdom. Instead of challenging his beliefs, Tommo's experience for the most part confirms it. When faced with something he cannot understand, he interprets it through his store of proverbial wisdom and, right or wrong, is smugly satisfied with his interpretation.

IN TERMS OF MELVILLE's use of proverbs, two impulses are apparent over his next several books. Sometimes he paraphrased well-worn proverbs for humorous effect; at others he revealed his fascination for sailor sayings and his desire to record them. In a way, these two impulses contradict one another. The first compelled Melville to reword proverbs deliberately, while the second had him keep traditional sayings intact. To that end he often used italics to separate the sailor proverbs from his own text, and thus further distinguished them as a separate mode of discourse. The sailor sayings Melville recorded in *Redburn* and *White-Jacket* help enliven the narrative, yet they seem motivated to some degree by a folklorist's desire to get them into print for posterity's sake. Melville performed his task well. His works constitute the only recorded references to many traditional sailor sayings.[5]

Reworking proverbs for humorous effect, Melville made them deliberately wordy and convoluted. *Omoo* and *Mardi* provide good examples. Nowadays we talk about someone getting up on the wrong side of the bed, but in Melville's day the proverb had cranky people get out of bed the wrong way. Describing Dr. Long Ghost's characteristic early-morning surliness, however, Melville wrote, "My long comrade was one of those, who, from always thrusting forth the wrong foot foremost when they rise, or committing some other indiscretion of the limbs, are more or less crabbed or sullen before breakfast" (*O* 226). At Melville's hand the proverbial phrase "to lose your head" becomes sheer delight. After telling how Samoa amputated his own arm in *Mardi*, the narrator explains that warriors in Varvoo commonly practice self-amputation; he then notes, "But, though thus beholden to no one for aught connected with the practice of surgery, they never cut off their own heads, that ever I heard; a species of amputation to which, metaphorically speaking, many would-be independent sort of people in civilized lands are addicted" (*M* 77).

Mardi's fictional setting hindered Melville's use of proverbs. Though he had recorded some quaint sailor sayings in *Omoo*, he could not really pursue his interest in sailor proverbs with *Mardi*. By detaching his narrator from the sailor's workaday world for a pleasure cruise around the Mardi archipelago, Melville also detached him from the sailor's verbal world. Paul Proverb went the way of Ned Ballad. Melville did find one outlet for his interest in proverbs within the pages of *Mardi*, however: he made some up. And why not? An imaginary voyage deserves imaginary proverbs. When King Media is reluctant to dine with some dwarfish, Caliban-like islanders, Babbalanja quotes "the old proverb—'Strike me in the face, but refuse not my yams'" and thereby compels King Media to take a seat at the table (*M* 573). Describing a way to live a rich, luxurious, pleasureful life, the Mardians say, "You are lodged like the king in Willamilla" (*M* 231).[6] Even Melville's manufactured proverbs, however, are tinged with irony. Though the king in Willamilla lives a luxurious life, tradition requires him to remain in Willamilla from the day he assumes the royal girdle until his death. At one level, to be lodged like a king in Willamilla means to live in luxury, but at another it means to be a prisoner for life.

Redburn and *White-Jacket* proved better forums for Melville to indulge in proverbs. Many of the sailor sayings he recorded in these two works are inherently ironic. Describing how sailors label parts of a ship according to features of the urban landscape and give themselves fictional addresses, he comments, "Sailors have a great fancy for naming things that way on shipboard. When a man is hung at sea, which is always done from one of the lower yard-arms, they say he *'takes a walk up Ladder-lane, and down Hemp-street'*" (R 82–83). Observing small fishing boats, he comments, "They were very small craft; and when I beheld them, I perceived the force of that sailor saying, intended to illustrate restricted quarters, or being *on the limits. It is like a fisherman's walk,* say they, *three steps and overboard*" (R 96). Discussing the education of midshipmen aboard a man-of-war, White-Jacket remarks, "As the only way to learn to command, is to learn to obey, the usage of a ship of war is such that the midshipmen are constantly being ordered about by the Lieutenants" (WJ 25). Another time White-Jacket observes that "the notorious lawlessness of the Commander has passed into a proverb, familiar to man-of-war's-men, *the law was not made for the Captain!*" (WJ 301). These are just a few of the numerous sailor sayings Melville recorded in *Redburn* and *White-Jacket,* yet they illustrate his predilection for both proverbs and irony.

IN LATER WORKS, Melville's use of proverbs sometimes takes on a darker quality. Not long after entering New York City with Isabel and Delly in a hired coach, Pierre Glendinning argues with their hack driver, who is unable to find the house Pierre had described. A policeman interposes, and Pierre agrees to have the driver unload their luggage in front of the watch-house. To explain to and ingratiate himself with the police officer, Pierre resorts to a proverb: "It is a rather strange accident, I confess, my friend, but strange accidents will sometimes happen." Pierre's, however, is a truncated version of a longer proverb. The policeman, whose suspicions have been aroused by the sight of a young man with two young women together in the city late at night, completes the proverb: "'In the best of families,' rejoined the other, a little ironically" (P 235). Caught in an awkward situation, Pierre uses the accidents-will-happen proverb to create conviviality between himself and the policeman, implying that his predicament was not uncommon. The policeman's response conveys his familiarity with the proverb, yet his ironic tone expresses his skepticism, questioning Pierre's status as being from the best of families.

"Hood's Isle and the Hermit Oberlus," the ninth sketch of "The Encantadas," tells the story of a vile miscreant banished to an island, where he kidnaps visiting sailors and makes them his slaves. When he finally has the opportunity, Oberlus steals a small boat to make his escape. Before leaving, however, he pins a note to the wall of his deserted hut; it contains the following postscript instructing the note's finder where to locate an "old fowl": "Do not kill it; be patient; I leave it setting; if it shall have any chicks, I hereby bequeathe them to you, whoever you may be. But don't count your chicks before they are hatched" (*PT* 168). The narrator next reveals what Oberlus had known when he wrote the postscript: the old fowl was "a starveling rooster, reduced to a sitting posture by sheer debility" (*PT* 169). Mean and spiteful to the end, Oberlus finds a way to perpetuate himself after he departs. Including a proverb as part of his own written discourse, Oberlus continues to provoke Hood's Isle visitors even after he makes his escape. The narrator's objectivity makes the episode effective and helps show how Melville's narrative style had matured since his early writings. Had Tommo been Oberlus's note-finder, he would have laughed off the sitting rooster with another proverb, "appearances are deceiving." The narrator here is never so reductive.

Like Oberlus's note-finder, Israel Potter encounters proverbs as part of a written text. In Paris, Potter has the opportunity to meet Benjamin Franklin and to spend an evening in his home. Franklin bids goodnight to Potter, leaving him with little but a guidebook to Paris and a copy of *The Way to Wealth* (or as it was also known, "Father Abraham's Speech"). The latter contains numerous sayings from Franklin's *Poor Richard's Almanac,* each tagged with the clause, "as Poor Richard says." *The Way to Wealth* had been published as a chapbook nearly a hundred years before Melville published *Israel Potter,* yet it remained in print in numerous languages.[7]

Taking the little book from the table, Potter opens it at random, a superstitious practice often used to predict the future. Though the Bible was the book most commonly used for divination, others could be pressed into service if need be.[8] In *The Confidence-Man,* for example, the man with the weed opens the sophomore's copy of Tacitus at random to read the ominous text, "In general a black and shameful period lies before me" (*CM* 25). Potter reads the randomly chosen passage, which contains several proverbs. The passage repels Potter, who exclaims, "Oh confound all this wisdom! It's sort of insulting to talk wisdom to a man like me. It's wisdom that's cheap, and it's fortune that's dear. That ain't in Poor Richard; but it ought to be" (*IP*

54). He slams down the pamphlet but soon has a change of heart and takes it up again. The second time he finds a proverb which appeals to him: "Ah, what's this Poor Richard says: 'God helps them that help themselves.' Let's consider that. Poor Richard ain't a Dunker, that's certain, though he has lived in Pennsylvania. 'God helps them that help themselves.' I'll just mark that saw, and leave the pamphlet open to refer to again.—Ah!" (*IP* 54).

John Paul Jones soon visits Potter's chamber, where he sees the copy of *The Way to Wealth* opened to the marked page: "'God helps them that help themselves.' That's a clincher. That's been my experience. But I never saw it in words before" (*IP* 61). As a written text, the proverb forcefully impresses Jones. He is so struck by the volume that he exclaims, "I must get me a copy of this, and wear it around my neck for a charm." Despite the facetious tone, Jones's words enhance the significance of Franklin's little book. Only the most powerful texts were so used. Often individual psalms were copied from the Bible and used as talismans, and sometimes pocket Bibles, prayer books, or books of black magic were carried as amulets.[9]

The same proverb is repeated twice more in *Israel Potter*. When Jones decides to rename his ship, Potter suggests *Poor Richard*. Jones finds the suggestion an inspired one and exclaims, "Poor Richard shall be the name, in honor to the saying, that 'God helps them that help themselves,' as Poor Richard says" (*IP* 115). They soon encounter an old Quaker woman preaching the biblical text, "The righteous shall rejoice when he seeth the vengeance. He shall wash his feet in the blood of the wicked." Her words are from the Book of Psalms (58.10), but Jones gives her a better text: "Now hear mine;—God helpeth them that help themselves, as Poor Richard says" (*IP* 118).

Nearly every time the proverb is invoked in *Israel Potter,* Franklin's text supplants the Bible. Potter first opens *The Way to Wealth* at random to help determine his future, a superstitious practice that more commonly required the Bible. Jones wants to use *The Way to Wealth* as an amulet, a role often fulfilled by biblical text. Jones further suggests that the proverb makes a better text for a sermon than does the Bible. The repetition of this proverb and its elevation above biblical text seems to make its validity unquestionable; ironically, however, when in fact Potter tries to help himself, as it enjoins, he ends up impoverished and trapped in London. Franklin's text renders the Bible powerless; Potter's experience, in turn, questions the validity of

Franklin's proverbial text. Brave and resourceful, with a chameleon-like ability to change identities to suit the situation, Israel Potter nevertheless lacks Tommo's store of proverbial wisdom. Deprived of both Scripture and proverbs, Potter is left with no text to guide his behavior.

THE DISTINCTIVE WAYS Melville used proverbs reveal his literary craftsmanship. Both the rarity of proverbs in *Pierre* and their frequency in *The Confidence-Man* demonstrate his careful diction. *Pierre,* set among the New England aristocracy and told by an omniscient, third-person narrator who devotes a considerable amount of prose to exploring his hero's thought processes, contains relatively few traditional sayings. Where they do occur, they are often elaborately paraphrased. Thus the proverb "It's always darkest before the dawn" becomes: "Glorified be his gracious memory who first said, The deepest gloom precedes the day. We care not whether the saying will prove true to the utmost bounds of things; sufficient that it sometimes does hold true within the bounds of earthly finitude" (*P* 172). *The Confidence-Man,* on the other hand, is set aboard the leveling vehicle of a Mississippi steamboat. Though also told in the third person, the work contains little exposition; instead, dialogue between passengers takes up most of the text. Proverbs are as appropriate to *The Confidence-Man* as they are inappropriate to *Pierre.*

In *The Confidence-Man* Melville twice used the proverbial phrase "wild goose chase." In Chapter 3, "In Which a Variety of Characters Appear," passengers question the authenticity of Black Guinea's deformities and demand documentary verification. Only when Black Guinea is unable to supply written evidence are they willing to accept oral testimony. He then lists several gentlemen who could vouch for him. In disbelief, the man with the wooden leg exclaims, "Wild goose chase!" Since the Black Guinea's list is a surrogate for a written document and, furthermore, roughly outlines the remainder of *The Confidence-Man,* Melville may be suggesting that the proverb applies to the entire book.

Fast-forward to the last chapter, "The Cosmopolitan Increases in Seriousness." In conversation with an old man late that evening, the cosmopolitan happens to cite a biblical passage that the old man initially fails to recognize. Eventually, the old man realizes that the cosmopolitan's text is from the Apocrypha. The old man shows him the word "Apocrypha" as it appears in a nearby Bible, using a proverb to explain himself: "Yes; and there's the word in black and white" (*CM* 243). Earlier, the barber had used the same proverb when he insisted that his agreement with the cosmopolitan "should be put in black and white" (*CM* 234), but the repetition of the phrase here is ironic, for it is applied to writing that is apocryphal: the word "Apocrypha" may be down in black and white, but its text, to use another proverbial phrase, may not be the gospel truth.

A young peddler interrupts their conversation, and the old man purchases an ingenious traveler's lock from him. Thrilled with the clever gadget, the old man uses a proverb to express himself: "This beats printing" (*CM* 246). Though less colorful than our modern equivalent ("This is the greatest thing since sliced bread"), the proverb says much about print culture, asserting as it does that moveable type was an invention with which all subsequent inventions could be proverbially compared. The use of this proverb is almost always ironic, of course, for few inventions, especially those drawn from an itinerant peddler's pack, actually excell printing.

The boy also sells the old man a *Counterfeit Detector,* one of several periodical publications available in Melville's America purporting to describe how to detect bogus currency. After the boy leaves, the old man devotes considerable effort to comparing the bills in his wallet against the *Counterfeit Detector.* The cosmopolitan attempts to dissuade him from the troublesome task, but the old man persists, stating:

> No; it's troublesome, but I think I'll keep it.—Stay, now, here's another sign. It says that, if the bill is good, it must have in one corner, mixed in with the vignette, the figure of a goose, very small, indeed, all but microscopic; and, for added precaution, like the figure of Napoleon outlined by the tree, not observable, even if magnified, unless attention is directed to it. Now, pore over it as I will, I can't see this goose. (*CM* 248–49)

Melville deliberately chose the currency's iconography so the cosmopolitan could characterize the old man's efforts as a "wild goose chase." The proverb is the third in the chapter to reflect print culture; it applies to the old man's use of one printed object, the *Counterfeit Detector,* to interpret another, the bill of currency. The cosmopolitan's use of the phrase is literal, not figurative, for the old man *is* looking for a goose. Taken together, all three proverbs question the value of print for expressing truth.

Occurring early in *The Confidence-Man* and repeated in the final chapter, the wild-goose proverb serves as a frame for most of the book. Its repetition parallels the Black Guinea's list of men who would vouch for him with the old man's counterfeit-detecting efforts. Since the Black Guinea's list roughly outlines the book itself and the old man's efforts show him searching a printed object for its masked signs, the proverb can be applied to the activity of reading *The Confidence-Man*. Is the reader's search for hidden signification, like the old man's, just another wild goose chase?

ANOTHER PROVERB MELVILLE used in his letter to Kate reappears in his later fiction. In the letter, "Handsome is, that handsome does" is expressed in an offhand manner, with little thought behind it. Having used the word "handsome" to characterize all women named Kate, Melville remembers and quotes the proverb. It did not really apply to women named Kate, for as Francis Grose had explained some years before, it was a proverb "frequently cited by ugly women."[10] Mrs. Primrose, wife of the vicar of Wakefield, said of her homely children, "They are as heaven made them—handsome enough, if they be good enough; for handsome is that handsome does."[11] When a horse in William T. Porter's *Quarter Race in Kentucky* is described as "heavy-bodied, hammer-headed, thin in the shoulder, bald-faced," yet fairly efficient, its owner says of her, "She aint no Wenus . . . but handsome is as handsome does."[12]

Melville reused the proverb in *Billy Budd*. When Billy spills his soup, Claggart remarks, "Handsomely done, my lad! And handsome is as handsome did it, too." When Claggart says "Handsomely done," he is being sarcastic (nowadays we say "Nice job!" to someone who commits an analogous blunder). The proverb "Handsome is as handsome does" has a built-in irony, in that it suggests that the unattractive can be made attractive by a polite, gracious, kind manner. As he composed *Billy Budd* Melville deliberately reworded the traditional proverb, however. He first wrote, "And handsome is as handsome does too!" Later he cancelled "does too" and above the cancelled words wrote: "did it too" (*BB* 328). With its tense changed to the past and the direct object "it" added, the sentence, unlike the traditional proverb, does not characterize a person's general behavior but refers to one particular act, Billy's spilling the soup. Applying the proverb to a Handsome Sailor, Melville reversed the irony; for, as Claggart says it, the phrase implies that handsomeness determines standards for behavior rather than, as the traditional proverb would have it, behavior for handsomeness. Billy, oblivious to "double meanings and insinuations," takes the proverb as an allusion to his status as a Handsome Sailor without comprehending its irony.

ONE MORE PROVERB BY WAY of conclusion: In both *Mardi* and *Moby-Dick* Melville mentioned the proverbial calm before the storm. Witnessing a huge volcanic eruption on Porpheero, Babbalanja contemplates the sometimes purifying and rejuvenating power of fire. "My lord," he says to King Media, "if calms breed storms, so storms calms; and all this dire commotion must eventuate in peace" (*M* 500). Babbalanja's words anticipate those of Ahab who, more eloquently, says, "But the mingled, mingling threads of life are woven by warp and woof: calms crossed by storms, a storm for every calm" (*MD* 492). The traditional proverb usually only mentions a calm *before* the storm, not after; Melville's modification suggests that the ironic juxtaposition of calm and storm was important to his own belief system.

When Melville considered retelling the story of Agatha Hatch, a story that would become his never-published *The Isle of the Cross*, he returned to the proverb. Working out some ideas in a letter to Nathaniel Hawthorne, Melville wrote, "Supposing the story to open with the wreck—then there must be a storm; & it were well if some faint shadow of the preceding *calm* were thrown forth to lead the whole" (*Co* 235). In *The Isle of the Cross,* the proverb not only may have been important as a verbal expression; it may have profoundly influenced the book's structure. We will never know.

· FOUR ·

Phantom
Sailors

While on a sailing voyage through the Mediterranean, Leigh Hunt hoped to hear some firsthand ghost stories from the sailors, but he came away from the experience greatly disappointed. Hunt later recalled:

> I tried to elicit some ghost stories of vessels, but could hear of nothing but the Flying Dutchman; nor did I succeed better on another occasion. This dearth of supernatural adventures is remarkable, considering the superstition of sailors. But their wits are none of the liveliest; the sea blunts while it mystifies; and the sailor's imagination, driven in, like his body, to the vessel he inhabits, admits only the petty wonders that come directly about him in the shape of storm-announcing fishes and birds. His superstition is that of a blunted and not of an awakened ignorance. Sailors had rather sleep than see visions.[1]

Unable to draw any stories from them beyond the widely known Flying Dutchman legend (motif E511), Leigh Hunt assumed that the sailors had no stories to tell. He failed to realize, however, that there may have been other reasons why he was unable to elicit stories. The class difference, first of all, would have made it difficult for them to associate with Hunt. Sailors often met the well educated or the well-to-do with belligerence. When Richard Henry Dana challenged one sailor's superstitious belief, for example, the sailor taunted him, "You think, 'cause you been to college, you know better than anybody."[2] And Dana had the advantage of sailing before the mast, an advantage Hunt did not have. Traveling as a passenger instead of a simple sailor further distanced him from the crew. Also, Hunt failed to realize that ghost stories had a time and place; they required specific conditions before they could be told. Leigh Hunt did not hear any good sailor ghost stories because he was unaware of the social contexts necessary.

Sailors generally told ghost stories after someone had died aboard ship. The stories, mainly personal legends, would often keep them awake through the night following a death. Otherwise they seldom told stories of phantom sailors. Icons of death—recall Queequeg's coffin—normally sent sailors scurrying away in superstitious dread, and talking about the dead when all aboard were alive and well similarly evoked superstitious fears of death. The fact that Hunt repeatedly heard the legend of the Flying Dutchman, a doomed craft most often sighted near Cape Horn that eternally sailed the seas and brought bad luck to any vessel answering its hails, suggests that either the legend belonged to a storytelling tradition separate from the postmortem repertoire or that it had become so commonplace that it had lost its ability to evoke wonder. The first possibility seems likelier. After all, Edgar Allan Poe had remarked that the legend of the Flying Dutchman possessed "all the rich *materiel* which a vigorous imagination could desire."[3]

Herman Melville understood what Leigh Hunt did not. Sailors "love marvels," he wrote, "and love to repeat them" (*M* 123). Melville also recognized the conditions necessary for storytelling aboard ship and frequently described the contexts of ghost-story telling. Indeed, he devoted more space to describing the storytelling context than to retelling ghost stories. Throughout his sea fiction Melville showed how various folk genres—burial customs, superstitions, personal narratives, tales, and legends—came together in performance.

OMOO GAVE MELVILLE his first opportunity to describe such a performance. Two sailors aboard the *Julia* die within an hour of one another. The first, stitched up in his hammock, is slipped into the sea without ceremony. The second death, coincidental though it may be (both men had been ill for some time), triggers the sailors into action, and they call for "additional ceremony" as well as a Bible or prayer book to carry out the burial service. A commonplace superstition among sailors was that committing a body to the sea without a proper burial ceremony will cause the deceased to haunt the place where he had died.[4] The second sailor's death affirms the bad luck betokened by their failure to follow traditional burial customs on the occasion of the first. In addition, the second death itself may presage further death to come. To stave off ill fortune and minimize the possibility of being haunted, the sailors take more care with the second corpse. With neither Bible nor prayer book aboard, they cannot comply precisely with the traditional custom by reading the burial service, so they improvise. A countryman of the deceased steps up, mutters something over the corpse, and makes the sign of the cross on the burial shroud before they commit the sailor's body to the sea.

The two deaths disturb the *Julia*'s crew members; they stay awake on deck until morning "relating to each other those marvelous tales of the sea which the occasion was calculated to call forth." The ship's carpenter tells a personal legend describing a voyage during which nearly half the crew died within a few days. Phantoms had appeared at the yardarm ends, and mysterious voices called aloud. The surviving crew members had consequently taken precautions, never ascending the rigging alone. Nonetheless, the carpenter, going aloft during a squall with a shipmate to furl the main topgallant sail, had been almost pushed from the rigging by an unseen hand, while his shipmate had a wet hammock "flirted in his face." After describing the carpenter's personal narrative in summary, the narrator skeptically explains, "Stories like these were related as gospel truths, by those who declared themselves eye-witnesses" (*O* 46).

At one point during this all-night storytelling session, the *Julia*'s Finnish sailor places his hand upon the horseshoe nailed to the foremast and prophesies that in less than three weeks fewer than one-quarter of the crew would remain aboard, an omen that many of the sailors interpret as a prophecy of death. Upon hearing the prediction a few chuckle in disbelief, but most are affected by it: "For several days a degree of quiet reigned among us, and allusions of such a kind were made to recent events, as could be attributed to no other cause than the Finn's omen" (*O* 47). Only when the remaining sick men on board begin to rally are the sailors' superstitious fears allayed.

With the episode aboard the *Julia*, Melville linked several folk genres into a cohesive pattern. A chance occurrence, the coincidental second death, activates superstitious fears and reminds the sailors of the traditional burial customs they had neglected. The death also serves as an omen of further death unless precautionary measures are taken. After the burial ceremony the sailors tell personal legends that incorporate traditional ghost-story motifs. The numerous legends encourage the Finn's prophecy and make it all the more convincing. Placing his hand upon the horseshoe, the Finn shows that the superstitious object could be much more than a lucky charm; for those gifted with second sight, the horseshoe serves as a conduit to the realm of the supernatural. The Finn's ominous prediction greatly influences the sailors' behavior until another chance occurrence, the recovery of the remaining invalids, minimizes their fear of imminent death.

The episode reinforces the social function of storytelling aboard ship. Even among the healthiest of sailors and the best of crews, death was an ever-present danger aboard nineteenth-century whaling vessels. Telling stories of phantoms allowed the sailor to cope with a shipmate's death, which might just as easily might have been his own. The storytelling session gave sailors an opportunity to bond with one another and share their concerns without having to admit to fear or to indulge in maudlin sentimentalism.

Such social and psychological associations pertain to any and all postmortem storytelling sessions, and Melville captures their mood. Yet a current of irony runs through his narration. The Finnish sailor, after all, is named "Van," a name that recalls Melville's youthful newspaper attack on a fellow member of the Philo Logos Society, Charles Van Loon: "In the *van* of these notable worthies stands pre-eminent, that silly and brainless *loon* who composed the article in your last week's paper" (*Co* 11). The superstitious Finn leads his fellow sailors into further superstition, and they willingly follow his lead. Being in the van does not necessarily mean being right, and a leader can take his followers the wrong way as easily as he can bring them the right way.

The narrator's superior tone, combined with the Finn's ironic name, undermines the ghost stories and their accompanying superstitions in *Omoo*. After thus discrediting the supernatural lore he describes, Melville's narrator curiously reasserts its validity—for the Finn's prediction does indeed come true. When several crew members refuse to work, they are taken off the *Julia*, put ashore, and confined to the calabooza. As the Finn predicted, fewer than one-quarter of the crew members remain on board. The rest do not die, as the sailors had understood the Finn's prediction to mean, but then again they had read too much into his prediction: he had never said they would die. Having the omen come true, Melville acknowledged the possibility of supernatural signs yet questioned man's ability to understand or interpret them. Melville's point is reminiscent of a query Emerson had made in his "Demonology" lecture less than ten years before: "Things are significant enough, Heaven knows, but the seer of the sign, where is he?"[5]

In *Redburn,* Melville more fully integrated the ghost-story-telling performance with his overall novel. In the course of the book, two particular incidents occur that might prompt ghost stories, but only the second does. Shortly after Wellingborough Redburn sails aboard the *Highlander,* one of the drunken sailors who has been brought aboard awakens and, apparently in the throes of *delirium tremens,* panics, runs shrieking across the deck, and dashes himself into the sea. Instead of inspiring a ghost-story-telling session, however, the crazy suicide incident encourages the other sailors to make fun of the greenhorn Redburn. They laugh at him for being frightened, call him a coward, and tell him to return inland, beyond all sight of water. When he in turn accuses them of fear and cowardice, they viciously berate him. Jackson, the vilest of the lot, tells Redburn to stay away from him or he will pitch him overboard.

The suicide was just the kind of event which could lead to a ghost-story-telling session. Since Redburn had never been to sea before, he knew no phantom sailor stories, so he could not have participated actively, though he might have simply listened to the others. Instead, the sailors use the suicide as an opportunity to initiate Redburn into sailor society. After witnessing his first death at sea, Redburn does not mask his fear or sublimate it through the process of storytelling; rather, he openly displays it. The other sailors rib him about the fear he expresses, but instead of laughing along with them and being a good sport, he strikes back, accusing them of cowardice. Finding young Redburn unwilling to participate in the fun, they ostracize him. The suicide, in other words, provides Redburn the opportunity to be indoctrinated into sailor society, but he refuses to take advantage of the opportunity and thus remains an outsider.

A similar death occurs on the return journey from Liverpool. Melville explicitly paralleled the two episodes. Introducing the later incident, Redburn explains, "It was destined that our departure from the English strand, should be marked by a tragical event, akin to the sudden end of the suicide, which had so strongly impressed me on quitting the American shore" (R 243). When Miguel Saveda, a sailor who had been brought aboard apparently in a catatonic state of drunkenness, does not rise for his duties, the men go to his bunk, where Jackson discovers he is dead. The corpse then spontaneously combusts.

They smother the flames in the blankets and hurry the dead man's body overboard without ceremony. Redburn describes his own reaction and subsequent behavior: "This event thrilled me through and through with unspeakable horror; nor did the conversation of the watch during the next four hours on deck, at all serve to soothe me" (*R* 245). Much like the double burial in *Omoo*, this particular incident prompts a lengthy storytelling session. Though the stories do nothing to allay Redburn's horror, he remains among the sailors during the four-hour period. Many of the other sailors aboard the *Highlander* recall similar occurrences. Redburn states, "And I heard Jackson say, that he had known of such things having been done before. But that a really dead body ever burned in that manner, I can not even yet believe. But the sailors seemed familiar with such things; or at least with the stories of such things having happened to others" (*R* 245). The contrasts between the early and late episodes allow the reader to see how Redburn has matured during the course of his first sailor voyage: no longer does he confront or castigate his fellow sailors, nor does he accuse them of fear. He has no stories to tell, but he sits entranced, listening to the legends of others for several hours.

Redburn comes away from his experience aboard the *Highlander* with a ghost story in his repertoire, for he can now tell the story of the spontaneous combustion of Miguel Saveda—and he does. Describing the episode in his narrative, Redburn explains that

> to the silent horror of all, two threads of greenish fire, like a forked tongue, darted out between the lips; and in a moment, the cadaverous face was crawled over by a swarm of worm-like flames.
>
> The lamp dropped from the hand of Max, and went out; while covered all over with spires and sparkles of flame, that faintly crackled in the silence, the uncovered parts of the body burned before us, precisely like a phosphorescent shark in a midnight sea.
>
> The eyes were open and fixed; the mouth was curled like a scroll, and every lean feature firm as in life; while the whole face, now wound in curls of soft blue flame, wore an aspect of grim defiance, and eternal death. Prometheus, blasted by fire on the rock.
>
> One arm, its red shirt-sleeve rolled up, exposed the man's name, tattooed in vermilion, near the hollow of the middle joint; and as if there was something peculiar in the painted flesh, every vibrating letter burned so white, that you might read the flaming name in the flickering ground of blue. (*R* 244)

The description shows that Redburn has mastered the art of telling horror stories. This personal legend incorporates traditional motifs, as the body catches fire of its own accord (motif F964.3.3) and flames issue from its mouth (motif E421.3.7).[6] The flaming tattoo further enhances the horror; burning text was generally associated with the devil.[7] The final image, therefore, suggests that Saveda's body has been taken by the devil.

The burning-corpse episode reverberates through the remainder of *Redburn.* Much like the two burials in *Omoo,* the incident and the stories that follow provoke superstitions. None of the *Highlander's* crew members, except Jackson, willingly lingers in the forecastle at noon or night. Instead of making merry there, they keep "their pleasantries for the watches on deck." Jackson, Redburn explains, "while the rest would be sitting silently smoking on their chests, or in their bunks, would look toward the fatal spot, and cough, and laugh, and invoke the dead man with incredible scoffs and jeers. He froze my blood, and made my soul stand still" (*R* 245–46).

The sailors' refusal to approach the place of the burning corpse is reminiscent of the carpenter's story in *Omoo.* All seem unwilling to risk meeting the ghost of Miguel Saveda—all, that is, except Jackson. During the remainder of the book Jackson seems almost to *become* Miguel Saveda's ghost. Having mastered the technique of horror, Redburn feels free to use it as he describes Jackson: "His aspect was damp and death-like; the blue hollows of his eyes were like vaults full of snakes; and issuing so unexpectedly from his dark tomb in the forecastle, he looked like a man raised from the dead" (*R* 295). With John Claggart and the hermit Oberlus, Jackson ranks among Melville's most memorable villains, but within the novel's context Jackson is a monster of his own making, for he helped teach young Redburn how to tell a tale of horror.

WHITE-JACKET ASSOCIATES several folk genres concerning death at sea. Soon after crew members aboard the *Neversink* fish up the ominous buoy that prefigures the death of a crew member, the ship's cooper drowns. The episode is based on a real event which occurred while Melville served aboard the *United States.*[8] Melville does not describe a subsequent storytelling session in *White-Jacket,* but, to be sure, they would have taken place aboard the *United States.* In *White-Jacket* the death, however, activates superstitions concerning the dead.

The next night White-Jacket ascends the main royal yard and, characteristically, remains there in a contemplative mood. Some sailors below soon cause him to make a near-fatal slip. Seeing a moving figure in white, they mistake him for the cooper's ghost (motif J1782.6). They hail and bid him to descend so they can test his corporeality, but he does not hear them. In fear, they lower the halyards, causing White-Jacket to slip. After recovering his balance and his wits, White-Jacket scrambles down, appearing to the men below "white as a hammock," a proverbial comparison that reinforces the ghost association and also recalls the carpenter's story in *Omoo*.

The hammock used as a burial shroud takes on further significance later in *White-Jacket*. Chapter 80, "The Last Stitch," describes a particular custom through the conversation of two old sailmakers, Ringrope and Thrummings. A long-standing burial tradition requires them to put the last stitch through the corpse's nose. Besides confirming that the person was truly dead, and making sure that the shroud would not detach itself from the body, the stitch fulfilled the superstitious purpose of ensuring that the dead man's ghost would not haunt the ship.[9] Thrummings, however, admits that though he always practiced the custom, the ghosts haunted him anyway:

> I never yet sewed up a shipmate but he spooked me arterward. I tell ye, Ringrope, these 'ere corpses is cunning. You think they sinks deep, but they comes up agin as soon as you sails over 'em. They lose the number of their mess, and their mess-mates sticks their spoons in the rack; but no good—no good, old Ringrope; they ar'n't dead yet. I tell ye, now, ten best-bower-anchors wouldn't sink this 'ere top-man. He'll be soon coming in the wake of the thirty-nine spooks what spooks me every night in my hammock—jist afore the mid-watch is called. Small thanks I gets for my pains; and every one on 'em looks so 'proachful-like, with a sail-maker's needle through his nose. I've been thinkin', old Ringrope, it's all wrong that 'ere last stitch we takes. Depend on't, they don't like it—none on 'em." (*WJ* 339)

Upon hearing this admission, White-Jacket interposes and suggests that the two old sea-undertakers abandon the custom. Thrummings is willing, but Ringrope is reluctant. "I'm agin all innovations," Ringrope says to White-Jacket. "It's a good old fashion, that last stitch; it keeps 'em snug, d'ye see, youngster. I'm blest if they could sleep sound, if it wa'n't for that. No, no, Thrummings! no innovations; I won't hear on't. I goes for the last stitch!" (*WJ* 339). Ringrope and Thrummings argue about it at length; eventually Ringrope is ordered elsewhere, and Thrummings is left to finish the job. Before leaving, Ringrope reminds him to finish the job properly: "But mind ye, take that 'ere last stitch, now; if ye don't, there's no tellin' the consekenses" (*WJ* 340). Though a humorous episode, "The Last Stitch" confirms the pattern Melville first outlined in *Omoo*. A death at sea prompts certain burial customs that lead to stories of the dead haunting the ship, which in turn confirm and reinforce superstitious beliefs.

IN 1850, SHORTLY AFTER *White-Jacket* had been completed and set in type, Melville set sail for England, taking a set of proof sheets to show prospective publishers in London. Two days into the journey, a man committed suicide by jumping overboard. After the incident, the captain told Melville that the suicide had been "the fourth or fifth instance he had known of people jumping overboard. He told a story of a man who did so, with his wife on deck at the time. As they were trying to save him, the wife said it was no use; & when he was drowned, she said 'there were plenty more men to be had'" (*J* 6). The coincidence between this real episode and the one he had described in the early pages of *Redburn* must have occurred to Melville, though he made no explicit comparison in his trip journal.

Aboard ship, the passengers were not enjoying themselves much. Nearly all were seasick that stormy evening, except Melville, the one passenger who was an experienced sailor. He wrote in his journal:

> By night, it blew a terrific gale, & we hove to. Miserable time! nearly every one sick, & the ship rolling, & pitching in an amazing manner. About midnight, I rose & went on deck. It was blowing horribly—pitch dark, & raining. The Captain was in the cuddy, & directed my attention 'to those fellows' as he called them, —meaning several 'Corposant balls' on the yard arms & mast heads. They were the first I had ever seen, & resembled large, dim stars in the sky. (*J* 6)

The captain's personification of the corposants, the pale balls of fire which sometimes appeared aboard ship during a storm, was not uncommon.

Also known as St. Elmo's fire, the corposants had considerable legendary import. Some said they represented the souls of dead shipmates. Among whalemen, tradition had it that the corposants were
spirits of sailors who had died aboard. They were associated with suicide by drowning, an association Melville's recent experience reinforced. Others believed that they presaged disaster. The corposants
were a common motif in such legends of phantom ships as that of the
Flying Dutchman.[10] Though Melville had never seen the corposants
before, he undoubtedly had heard stories of them as a sailor. Furthermore, some of his favorite literary works mentioned them: Burton's
Anatomy of Melancholy, Camoens's *Lusiad,* and Shakespeare's *Tempest.* In *The Tempest* Ariel explains to Prospero that he appeared aboard
the storm-tossed ship in the guise of the corposants:

> I boarded the King's ship; now on the beak,
> Now in the waist, the deck, in every cabin,
> I flam'd amazement. Sometime I'd divide,
> And burn in many places; on the topmast,
> The yards and boresprit, would I flame distinctly,
> Then meet and join. Jove's lightning, the precursors
> O' th' dreadful thunder-claps, more momentary
> And sight-outrunning were not; the fire and cracks
> Of sulphurous roaring the most mighty Neptune
> Seem to beseige, and make his bold waves tremble,
> Yea, his dread trident shake.
> (*The Tempest,* 1.ii.196–205)

Melville's admission to his journal that he had never seen the
corposants verifies their rarity and explains why he had made no literary use of them beyond a brief reference in *Mardi.* In that book the
wanderers encounter Nulli, a character representing John C. Calhoun,
whom the narrator describes as "a cadaverous, ghost-like man" with
wondrous eyes "bright, nimble, as the twin Corposant balls, playing
about the ends of ships' royal-yards in gales" (*M* 532). In *Israel Potter*
Melville again used the corposants as a simile, in a description of
John Paul Jones during the fight between the *Bon Homme Richard*
and the *Serapis:* he "flew hither and thither like the meteoric
corposant-ball, which shiftingly dances on the tips and verges of ships'
rigging in storms. Wherever he went, he seemed to cast a pale light

on all faces" (*IP* 126). Not long after seeing the corposants for himself, however, Melville realized that the phenomenon had far greater imaginative and literary potential than a clever simile. The result was "The Candles," visually the most striking chapter in *Moby-Dick*.

Aboard the *Pequod* the light of the corposants enchants the crew, "all their eyes gleaming in that pale phosphorescence," and "while lit up by the preternatural light, Queequeg's tattooing burned like Satanic blue flames on his body" (*MD* 506). The image recalls Melville's description of the flaming tattoo of the body of Miguel Saveda in *Redburn*. Ahab encourages the men to look toward the light: "Look up at it; mark it well; the white flame but lights the way to the White Whale!" (*MD* 507).

In *Moby-Dick* the corposants appear at the top of each mast and the tips of all the yardarms. The sight of one light was generally considered bad luck, while the sight of two was good luck; the recorded lore says nothing about so many lights. Stubb first takes the corposants as a sign of good luck, an interpretation largely motivated by wishful thinking, for he hardly seems to believe it himself. Many superstitions were associated with the lights' movement: if they moved around the ship, it was a sign of bad weather; when seen aloft, the lights represented good luck; but seen at deck level, the lights were a bad sign. If the lights ascended from the prow, it was a good sign, but if they descended from the masthead, it was a bad one.[11] As Agath relates the story of his doomed vessel in *Clarel*, the corposants appear above and then descend:

> Corposants on yard-arms did burn,
> Red lightning forked upon the stern.
> (*Cl* 3.12.93–94)

The corposants first appear aboard the *Pequod* aloft, so Stubb's interpretation of them as good luck has some basis in superstition, but before long Ahab takes hold of the lightning links, virtually daring the light to descend. Sure enough, it does, enveloping Ahab's newly forged harpoon, from which emanates "a levelled flame of pale, forked fire." The light had descended from the masthead and was now at deck. The superstitions were pretty clear on this point: the descent from the masthead meant bad luck, and the light seen at deck level also meant bad luck. Starbuck recognizes that Stubb's initial inter-

pretation of good luck was wrong and that the downward movement of the corposants is ill omened. He attempts to discourage Ahab
from his pursuit. Ishmael explains, "As the silent harpoon burned
there like a serpent's tongue, Starbuck grasped Ahab by the arm—
'God, God is against thee, old man; forbear! 't'is an ill voyage!'" (*MD*
508). Ahab dashes the lightning links to the deck, snatches the burning harpoon, and waves it like a torch among his men. As any superstitious sailor knew, to have the pale light of the corposants thrown
upon one's face was fatal. Ahab's gesture turns all his men—save for
his chronicler, Ishmael—to phantom sailors.

FIVE

Tall Talk and
Tall Tales

Few experiences more widely separated the sailor from the land-lubber than rounding Cape Horn. The Cape's ferocious winds, slashing rain, bitter cold, and typhoon-sized waves were phenomena that only those who had endured them could truly understand. Sailors generally resented landlubbers who assumed knowledge of their work without firsthand experience. In "Prudence," Emerson asserted that though the sailor may buffet a storm all day, "his health renews itself as vigorous a pulse under the sleet, as under the sun of June." Reading the assertion in his copy of Emerson's *Essays,* Herman Melville wrote in the margin, "To one who has weathered Cape Horn as a common sailor what stuff all this is."[1] Melville himself had described rounding Cape Horn in *White-Jacket,* yet the attitude his narrator takes toward his readers in that work differs considerably from Melville's personal response to Emerson. Prior to his vivid description of sailing around Cape Horn (the finest in the language) White-Jacket tells a tall tale to convey the coldness of the Cape. It is so cold there, White-Jacket informs his readers, that "any man could have undergone amputation with great ease, and helped take up the arteries himself" (*WJ* 101). Lies about cold weather were common to tall-tale tradition (motif X1620), but far from belittling his stay-at-home readers who have never experienced such intense cold, White-Jacket's tale seems ingratiating.

Melville's use of the tall tale often mirrors the way the tall tale works in the oral culture. Within its social context, the tall tale normally serves to reinforce the identity of a folk group, excluding outsiders and strengthening the bond among insiders. Notwithstanding, it also offers outsiders the opportunity to be initiated into a folk group: they need only understand the humor of the tall tale, accept it, and go along with whatever lies they are told, no matter how outrageous. The outsider who does not recognize the tale's humor or does not appreciate it will remain an outsider. Occasionally, however, as Carolyn Brown has observed, the tall tale can establish a "temporary intimacy between strangers because it allows the perceptive listener—though not a candidate for initiation—to see and understand a part of the world of the narrator."[2] White-Jacket's tall tale allows those who will never sail beyond Cape May, let alone Cape Horn, to appreciate and understand the sailor's world, a world where the weather can get so severe that the only way to cope with it is by humorously exaggerating its severity all the more.

White-Jacket's tall tale does not necessarily mark an advance in Melville's literary use of folklore, however, for he had included tall tales in his writings since the early pages of *Typee*. While Melville greatly refined his use of other folk genres from one book to the next, his mastery of the tall tale had been obvious from the start of his career as an author. Melville integrated tall talk within his written discourse so well that many contemporary readers hesitated to accept *Typee* as fact.[3] Some thought that the whole book was more or less a tall tale. The *Morning Courier and New-York Enquirer*, for instance, called *Typee* "a piece of Munchausenism,—from beginning to end."[4]

The reviewer, of course, refers to Baron Munchausen, whose *Adventures and Travels* had earned him a reputation as the most famous liar in the history of travel writing and had established a benchmark for literary lying. Subsequent travel narratives of questionable veracity were often compared to his work. Before *Typee*, Edgar Allan Poe's *Narrative of Arthur Gordon Pym* had been likened to Munchausen's *Travels*.[5] Melville probably knew Munchausen's book in one form or another from his childhood. First published in English during the late eighteenth century, the work had gone through many British and American editions over the next several decades, including greatly abbreviated chapbook versions for young readers. Among several chapbook editions published during the 1820s was Solomon King's 1828 New York edition, *The Surprising Adventures of the Renowned Baron Munchausen*.[6]

While Munchausen's work probably introduced Melville to literary lying, he had plenty of opportunity to hear and repeat tall tales. Even before he reached the Marquesas, he had demonstrated his storytelling ability. Richard Tobias Greene later recalled Melville spinning yarns aboard the *Acushnet*, before the two deserted the ship together (*Co* 686). Melville's sailor experiences gave him ample opportunity to gratify and enhance his predilection for tall talk. By the time he sat down to write *Typee,* he had rehearsed the story of his adventures orally so many times that it hardly seems unusual that the written version frequently gives the impression of an oral tale. As Melville began his writing career, the tall tale was a mode of discourse he already had polished to a high sheen.

By no means do Melville's tall tales always come from the narrator's point of view, as does White-Jacket's tall tale about the coldness of the Cape. From Tommo through Ishmael, Melville's fictional narrators relate tall talk in many different ways. Occasionally they present the tall talk of others, using what Gérard Genette might call "direct discourse."[7] By presenting another's tales as direct quotations, the narrator casts himself in the listener's role and thus is able to describe how he had reacted to the tales as he had heard them. More often, Melville's narrators present the tall talk of others indirectly, changing the narrative point of view, putting what they had heard into their own words and supplying interpretive comments. Such indirect discourse allows the narrator to distance himself from the tall tale, to convey tall talk to his readers without becoming a tall talker himself. Indirect discourse did not always create such distancing, however. By framing the tall talk of another within sympathetic and appreciative comments, the narrator could create a camaraderie between himself and the tall talker. Often Melville's narrators, like White-Jacket, become tall talkers themselves, placing their readers into the listener's role and leaving them to accept or reject the lies told.

THE FIRST CHAPTER OF *Redburn* provides a fine example of tall talk conveyed as direct discourse. In terms of its overall narrative structure, *Redburn* is a story told by a well-seasoned sailor recalling his youth. As Wellingborough Redburn describes the things that had inspired him to go to sea, he remembers having seen a man who had traveled through many faraway lands and had established a fair reputation as a travel writer. (The character is based on John Lloyd Stephens.) His aunt, attending church with him one Sunday, had pointed the man out and told him a tall tale to explain the traveler's unusual facial appearance.[8] Redburn frames his aunt's tale with a prefatory description of the man and concludes it by describing his own reactions.

I very well remembered staring at a man myself, who was pointed out to me by my aunt one Sunday in Church, as the person who had been in Stony Arabia, and passed through strange adventures there, all of which with my own eyes I had read in the book which he wrote, an arid-looking book in a pale yellow cover.

"See what big eyes he has," whispered my aunt, "they got so big, because when he was almost dead with famishing in the desert, he all at once caught sight of a date tree, with the ripe fruit hanging on it."

Upon this, I stared at him till I thought his eyes were really of an uncommon size, and stuck out from his head like those of a lobster. I am sure my own eyes must have magnified as I stared. When church was out, I wanted my aunt to take me along and follow the traveler home. But she said the constables would take us up, if we did; and so I never saw this wonderful Arabian Traveler again. But he long haunted me; and several times I dreamt of him, and thought his great eyes were grown still larger and rounder; and once I had a vision of the date tree. (*R* 5–6)

By conveying his aunt's words as a direct quotation instead of paraphrasing them, Redburn allows the reader to experience her tale as he first had. The aunt's relationship to the tall tale is not entirely clear, however. She may have heard it herself and not recognized it as a tall tale, and thus be repeating it to her nephew as truth. On another level, she may be cognizant of the tall tale and telling it to her nephew to offer him an opportunity for initiation, the chance to become part of her adult world—a world filled with hard-working churchgoers who nod and hate trespassers. Young Redburn does not recognize her explanation as a tall tale. Instead, he believes what she says, scrutinizes the man all the more, and then expresses his desire to follow him home. If her tall tale is an attempt to bring Redburn into her world, instead he longs to enter the traveler's fantastic world, where anything could happen. Her adult world is a world of the conventional—home, duty, responsibility—whereas the traveler's is one of carefree adventure surrounded by eye-popping scenery. Small wonder he resists her attempt at initiation.

WHILE *REDBURN* IS AN older man's story of his youth, *Omoo* is told from the point of view of a young man with literary ambitions. It describes his fairly recent sailor adventures for an audience of armchair travelers, readers who appreciate thrilling adventure stories as long as they can read them surrounded by shelves filled with gilt morocco. Wanting very much to include the kinds of tall tales that had given *Typee* so much charm yet also wanting to avoid accusations of Munchausenism from the reviewers, Melville included tall tales within *Omoo* but had his narrator assume a superiority over them. For the most part, the *Omoo* narrator conveys the tall talk of others as indirect discourse. The approach gives him an opportunity to describe former associates—sailors, native islanders, and South Pacific drifters—while identifying with his urbane readers.

The tall tales start early in the book. Shortly after the *Julia* rescues him, the narrator describes the provisions aboard ship. The pickled meat leaves much to be desired. He explains, "When opened, the barrels of pork looked as if preserved in iron rust, and diffused an odor like a stale ragout. The beef was worse yet; a mahogany-colored fibrous substance, so tough and tasteless, that I almost believed the cook's story of a horse's hoof with the shoe on having been fished up out of the pickle of one of the casks" (*O* 13–14). Here the narrator neither quotes the cook nor describes his tall talk within its interpersonal context. Instead he first expresses disbelief and then quickly paraphrases the cook's story. Later, when the mate tells stories of whales so tame that they are too frightened to resist capture, the narrator similarly asserts that he did not believe such stories (*O* 35). By retelling tall tales through the use of indirect discourse and framing them with skeptical comments, the narrator preempts any objections his readers may have as to the book's veracity. Making his narrator a skeptic, Melville created a literary persona his readers could appreciate.

The most extended tall tale in *Omoo* similarly combines skepticism with indirect discourse in order to distance the narrator from his subject while bringing him closer to his readers. Before retelling a story he had heard from Tonoi, an old island chief, the narrator places it in the realm of the fantastic by stating that it "had a spice of the marvelous." He then deliberately evokes the language of the fairy tale by beginning the story with the formulaic opening, "Once upon a time." Furthermore, he tells the story in the third person instead of retaining Tonoi's first person, thus keeping greater narrative control.

> Once upon a time, he was going over the hills with a brother—now no more—when a great bull came bellowing out of a wood, and both

took to their heels. The old chief sprang into a tree; his companion, flying in an opposite direction, was pursued, and in the very act of reaching up to a bough, trampled under foot. The unhappy man was then gored—tossed in the air—and finally run away with on the bull's horns. More dead than alive, Tonoi waited till all was over, and then made the best of his way home. The neighbors, armed with two or three muskets, at once started to recover, if possible, his unfortunate brother's remains. At nightfall, they returned without discovering any trace of him; but the next morning, Tonoi himself caught a glimpse of a bullock, marching across the mountain's brow, with a long dark object borne aloft on his horns. (O 210)

Mardi's tall talk sometimes occurs in the narrative in this way. The *Mardi* narrator, who has taken the name Taji since arriving thither, describes a surgical operation Samoa the Upoluan had performed on a local diver who had cracked open his skull. The reader is already familiar with Samoa's surgical skill, for earlier in the book he had amputated his own arm, a surgery accompanied by the rather tall generalization that it sometimes took a native warrior several days to saw off one of his own limbs. The fact that the surgeon now has only one arm gives this second operation an even greater tall-tale quality. After removing bits of broken skull, Samoa places a cocoanut shell fragment in the vacancy, a technique known as trepanning. All admire his skill until Babbalanja wonders whether the patient had survived the operation. They double-check, only to discover that the diver is dead.

Samoa's surgery looks forward to "The Operation" in *White-Jacket*, one of the finest pieces of dark humor Melville, or anyone, ever wrote. Both the surgery in *Mardi* and that in *White-Jacket* end with hearty congratulations; the patient's death in each scarcely affects the pride the surgeon takes in his skill. Furthermore, one-armed Samoa anticipates Cadwallader Cuticle, the skeleton-like doctor in *White-Jacket*, sans teeth, sans eye, sans wig.

After both operations, the two surgeons each tell tall tales themselves. Dr. Cuticle's occurs in the narrative as direct discourse. He recalls a case where a bullet entered a man's Adam's apple, "ran completely round the neck, and, emerging at the same hole it had entered, shot the next man in the ranks" (*WJ* 263). In *Mardi* Samoa tells what Taji characterizes as a "traveller's tale." The tale belongs to the type (AT 660) "The Three Doctors," and it incorporates traditional motifs which tell how skillful surgeons remove and replace vital organs (motif F668.1) and how a man's organs are replaced with an animal's (motif X1721.2).[9] Retelling Samoa's tale, Taji uses the same approach the narrator in *Omoo* had used to retell Tonoi's story, for he puts it in the third person and uses the identical opening formula:

> Once upon a time, during his endless sea-rovings, the Upoluan was called upon to cobble the head of a friend, grievously hurt in a desperate fight of slings.
>
> Upon examination, that part of the brain proving as much injured as the cranium itself, a young pig was obtained; and preliminaries being over, part of its live brain was placed in the cavity, the trepan accomplished with a cocoanut shell, and the scalp drawn over and secured.
>
> This man died not, but lived. But from being a warrior of great sense and spirit, he became a perverse-minded and piggish fellow, showing many of the characteristics of his swinish grafting. He survived the operation more than a year; at the end of that period, however, going mad, and dying in his delirium. (*M* 298–99)

The story told, Taji continues to other islands and adventures. Some hundred and fifty pages later, he attends the martial games at Diranda. Before a ritualized combat requiring two groups of fifty men to battle one another with single sticks, a priest leads out one of the warrior groups. Taji describes the procession: "In advance marched a priest, bearing an idol with a cracked cocoanut for a head,—Krako, the god of Trepans" (*M* 447). The detail, brief as it is, marks a shift from *Omoo*, for it shows one character's tall tale influencing the narrative as a whole. The distinctions between the lie and the truth blur. The reader does not know whether to accept the priest's idol as part of the novel's imaginary world or to recognize it as a deliberate lie on the narrator's part.

IT IS POSSIBLE FOR THE narrator to convey the tall talk of others through indirect discourse without removing himself too far from his subject. Ishmael does it. Consider his description of Nantucket:

> Some gamesome wights will tell you that they have to plant weeds there, they don't grow naturally; that they import Canada thistles;

that they have to send beyond seas for a spile to stop a leak in an oil cask; that pieces of wood in Nantucket are carried about like bits of the true cross in Rome; that people there plant toadstools before their houses, to get under the shade in summer time; that one blade of grass makes an oasis, three blades in a day's walk a prairie; that they wear quicksand shoes, something like Laplander snow-shoes; that they are so shut up, belted about, every way inclosed, surrounded, and made an utter island of by the ocean, that to their very chairs and tables small clams will sometimes be found adhering, as to the backs of sea turtles. (*MD* 63)

Lies about remarkable land features were common to traditional tall tales (motif X1510).[10] So too were stories of great mushrooms (motif X1424) and lies about remarkable soil (motif X1530). Though Ishmael attributes such tall talk to others, he clearly delights in it. Instead of expressing his disbelief, he simply catalogues the tall tales and attributes them to "gamesome wights." The epithet suggests Ishmael's recognition of the playfulness of those who tell such lies. Elsewhere, he enlarges upon the idea of gamesomeness.[11] Describing a particular type of porpoise, he coins the name "Huzza Porpoise," explaining, "If you yourself can withstand three cheers at beholding these vivacious fish, then heaven help ye; the spirit of godly gamesomeness is not in ye" (*MD* 143–44). His gamesome tone places him much closer to his source than, say, the narrator to the cook in *Omoo*. Furthermore, the epithet suggests that Ishmael recognizes the tall-tale quality of the geographic descriptions yet has no intention of denying them. A gamesome wight himself, he appreciates their humor and makes it part of his narrative.

A similar example occurs later in the book. When the *Pequod* meets the *Bachelor*, the crew learns that the other vessel is heading homeward, with every cask on board filled with oil. The *Bachelor*'s crew describes to the *Pequod*'s their enormous success. Ishmael states that "it was humorously added, that the cook had clapped a head on his largest boiler, and filled it; that the steward had plugged his spare coffee-pot and filled it; that the harpooneers had headed the sockets of their irons and filled them; that indeed everything was filled with sperm, except the captain's pantaloon pockets, and those he reserved to thrust his hands into, in self-complacent testimony of his entire satisfaction" (*MD* 494). Much like the gamesome wights living on

Nantucket, the *Bachelor*'s crew enjoys their situation and exaggerates its notable qualities.

MELVILLE INCORPORATED TALL TALK WITHIN his writings most thoroughly when he made his narrator a tall talker and thus placed his readers into the listener's role. He occasionally used the technique in *Redburn* and *White-Jacket*, but he used it most often in *Typee* and *Moby-Dick*. Two key factors distinguish the tall talk in *Typee* and *Moby-Dick*, however. First, Tommo's tall tales are much less self-conscious than Ishmael's. The tales Melville himself told about his South Sea adventures before he wrote the book, one gets the impression, differed little in tone and content from Tommo's. Secondly, the subject matter of Tommo's tall tales differs from that of Ishmael's. This distinction may seem so simple that it hardly needs mentioning, yet a tall tale's setting and content greatly affect the relationship between its teller and the listener. Tommo's tall tales are traveler's tales; he tells stories about things he had encountered in his travels to the antipodes. Some concern activity aboard ship, while others are set on faraway islands, but all stem from the experience of a South Seas whaleman-adventurer. Ishmael's whaling adventures often form the basis for his tall tales—but not always. Sometimes he sets his tall tales much closer to home.

Emphasizing the length of a whaling voyage, Tommo asserts, "Some long-haired, bare-necked youths, who, forced by the united influences of Captain Marryat and hard times, embark at Nantucket for a pleasure excursion to the Pacific, and whose anxious mothers provide them with bottled milk for the occasion, often times return very respectable middle-aged gentlemen" (*T* 21). Later, describing the conjugation of verbs in Hawaii, Tommo explains, "The intricacy of these dialects is another peculiarity. In the Missionary College at Lahainaluna, on Mowee, one of the Sandwich Islands, I saw a tabular exhibition of a Haw[a]iian verb, conjugated through all its moods and tenses. It covered the side of a considerable apartment, and I doubt whether Sir William Jones himself would not have despaired of mastering it" (*T* 225). These are but two examples of Tommo's tall talk. There are many others, but all, or nearly all, reflect life in the South Pacific. Tommo's tall tales function the same way as White-Jacket's Cape Horn tall tale: they establish a "temporary intimacy" between narrator and reader that allows the reader to catch a glimpse of the Pacific adventurer's world.

Ishmael offers his readers something which Tommo does not. Though armchair travelers can never hope to enter Tommo's antipodean world, they can become a part of Ishmael's. This is not to say that they can become a part of his whaling world, though the book occasionally had such an effect on impressionable youths.[12] Rather, they can enter Ishmael's intellectual world, a world that can be as full of excitement and adventure as the South Pacific. Ishmael's relationship to Nantucket's gamesome wights early in the book gives readers a pattern to follow. If they recognize his tall tales and appreciate them as such, he will welcome their company gladly.

At one point Ishmael hypothesizes that the whale's spout is nothing but mist, and he uses the hypothesis to assert the sperm whale's dignity, sublimity, and profundity. For proof, he seeks analogues. Ultimately, he gets to himself as an example:

> While composing a little treatise on Eternity, I had the curiosity to place a mirror before me; and ere long saw reflected there, a curious involved worming and undulation in the atmosphere over my head. The invariable moisture of my hair, while plunged in deep thought, after six cups of hot tea in my thin shingled attic, of an August noon; this seems an additional argument for the above supposition. (*MD* 374)

Whereas Tommo's tall tales are set in the South Pacific, Ishmael's tall tale here is set in the civilized world, a place covered with a roof and filled with pen, paper, and ink—in other words, the natural habitat of armchair travelers and literati. Even the deepest thinkers and the most incorrigible tea drinkers had to know that thought could not make one's head steam. With this tall tale, as well as others—elsewhere Ishmael explains that he was keeping a part of his body tattoo-free to save space for a poem he was writing—Melville offered his readers lies that they could not help but recognize as such.

Though Melville made Tommo a master of the tall tale in *Typee*, he backed away from tall tales in *Omoo*. Gradually, though, his narrators again talk tall, and White-Jacket is second only to Ishmael as a tall-tale teller. The key difference between the way Melville used tall talk in *Omoo* and *Moby-Dick* signals one key difference between those two books. In *Omoo* the narrator skeptically retells the tales of others, adjusting his voice to suit his stay-at-home readers. In *Moby-Dick* Ishmael deliberately refuses to temper his voice to make it more compatible with refined readers; instead, he offers them a challenge. Whereas Tommo and White-Jacket give their readers but a temporary glimpse of their world, Ishmael offers his readers more. He offers them an opportunity for initiation. In *Moby-Dick* the relationship between narrator and reader closely parallels the relationship between a tall-tale teller and his listener in the oral culture. Ishmael's readers need only recognize the humor of his tall tales and go along with them in order to be initiated into his world, the world of the mind.

SIX

Redburn *and the* *Chapbook*

P reserved in a vault at the bottom of a long, dark, narrow stone staircase lies Mardi's collection of ancient and curious manuscripts. As Taji recalls the descent, he compares himself to Giovanni Battista Belzoni, the explorer of Egyptian pyramids. The comparison prepares the reader to expect a cache of precious goodies, a collection of highly wrought literature worthy of the ages, but the manuscript titles Taji lists by genre—brave old chronicles, Tarantula books, metaphysical treatises, popular literature—hardly seem like classics. Instead, they sound much like titles of books widely read and sometimes revered in Melville's America. The episode is an amusing, though transparent, lampoon of contemporary reading tastes. Melville's satiric targets are readers who confuse the best-liked books of the day with the books that will endure the ages, readers who mistakenly see a literary work's contemporary popularity as an indication of its lasting value.

That Melville included a work of "popular literature" among the list of titles heightens the irony, for the popular book, or chapbook, was not intended to be preserved for posterity but to be read, shared, and reread until it fell apart, at which time it was used for waste paper.[1] In the dedicatory epistle to *Israel Potter,* Melville playfully described his tattered copy of Israel Potter's chapbook autobiography as "forlornly published on sleazy gray paper" and "rescued by the merest chance from the rag-pickers" (*IP* vii).

Chapbooks, nearly coeval with the printing press, gradually encompassed a wider variety of literary genres over the centuries. The earliest chapbooks were mainly limited to traditional romances and legends, greatly condensed and simplified—*Fortunatus, Reynard the Fox,* and *The Seven Champions of Christendom,* to name a few—but after the sixteenth century, other kinds of works were published in chapbook formats. Histories, travels, and biographies, greatly abbreviated and simplified, appeared as chapbooks. Occult books, which had long circulated in manuscript, began to be cheaply printed and clandestinely distributed. Didactic books, often collections of adages culled from larger works, became an important part of the cheap print trade. Benjamin Franklin's *Way to Wealth,* for example, is early America's most important contribution to the international chapbook tradition. By the end of the eighteenth century, the sensational crime story had become one of the most popular chapbook genres.

The popular work Taji finds in the Mardian vault is entitled *A Most Sweet, Pleasant, and Unctuous Account of the Manner in Which Five-and-Forty Robbers Were Torn Asunder by Swiftly-Going Canoes* (*M* 383). Melville's mock-title nicely captures the titles of the sensational crime stories. The chapbook Taji finds tells a story of not just two or three robbers but forty-five of them. Instead of focusing on their crime, the book concentrates on their sanguineous demise. Despite the robbery and gore, the title implies, a theme of providential justice runs through the story: the robbers' end, though gruesome, is meet and right—they were, after all, robbers.

Chapbooks experienced further changes during the early decades of the nineteenth century. Didactic works, crime stories, and occult books continued to be printed in chapbook format for adults to read, but traditional romances and legends, while remaining in print as chapbooks, largely became children's books. Melville's writings contain allusions to both cheap crime books and children's chapbooks. In *The Confidence-Man,* for instance, one peddler hawks "the lives of Meason, the bandit of Ohio, Murrel, the pirate of the Mississippi, and the brothers Harpe, the Thugs of the Green River country, in Kentucky" (*CM* 4). Though the bandits Melville mentions were real, he does not necessarily refer to any particular chapbooks. His allusions to children's chapbook stories, on the other hand, often refer to actual chapbooks, books that for the most part have escaped scholarly attention.

The chapbook references in Melville's writings help clarify the otherwise fuzzy outlines of his boyhood reading. *Guy of Warwick,* a work he alluded to in *White-Jacket* (284), was a centuries-old romance, published in multiple editions during his childhood.[2] As a boy he almost surely read *The History of Blue Beard.* He mentions it in *Typee* (205), and chapbook editions were published in Albany, Cooperstown, and New Haven during his youth.[3] A copy of *The History of Goody*

Two-Shoes, a work Melville mentions in "Hawthorne and His Mosses" (*PT* 251), survives among his books.[4] *The History of Sinbad the Sailor* (*IP* 166; *Cl* 236, 306) was also available as a chapbook during Melville's boyhood.[5] *Jack the Giant-Killer,* a long-popular chapbook story mentioned in *Typee* (205), appeared separately in chapbook format during Melville's childhood and was often published in contemporary collections of children's stories. (Six-year-old Malcolm Melville attended a fancy-dress picnic in 1855 as Jack the Giant Killer.)[6] Besides *The Surprising Adventures of the Renowned Baron Munchausen,* New York publisher Solomon King issued other chapbook editions that Melville likely read in his boyhood: *Valentin and Orson,* a work he alluded to in *The Confidence-Man* (125–26), and *The Remarkable Life of Dr. Faustus.*[7] Though literary historians nearly always assume Melville's references to Faust are references to either Goethe or Marlowe, chances are that Melville first encountered the Faustus story the same way Goethe and Marlowe had, in its chapbook form. A chapbook story Melville alluded to in *Israel Potter* (47) and "The Apple-Tree Table" (*PT* 378), *The Famous Historie of Friar Bacon,* was often appended to editions of *Dr. Faustus.*[8] Though Melville likely had read Daniel Defoe's *Robinson Crusoe* in its entirety before he wrote *Typee,* a work to which it was often compared, he would have encountered Crusoe first in chapbook format during his childhood.[9] In the surviving draft pages of *Typee* (at the New York Public Library), Melville mentioned a popular religious tract, Mary Martha Sherwood's *Little Henry and His Bearer.*[10] Pierre Glendinning reads a "little history" about the French Revolution in his youth (*P* 75); young Melville may have read *The French Revolution,* one of Robert Dale Owens's "Popular Tracts."[11] Alan Melvill kept many classic works of literature finely bound at his New York City home during the 1820s, but the earliest books his son Herman read would have been chapbooks.

TAJI'S VISIT TO THE manuscript-filled catacombs in *Mardi* reveals Melville's interest in the relationship between popular literature and the literary classic, but *Mardi,* as Melville conceived it, proved a difficult forum for pondering the vicissitudes of print culture. In other words, it was hard to explore the world of print by imagining a culture without print. The real-world setting of his next book, however, allowed him to juxtapose popular literature with elite literature and compare their values. The ultimate impression of popular literature that *Redburn* provides, however, is ambivalent.

In the first chapter, Wellingborough Redburn recalls the sumptuous world of his father's library as well as his boyhood reading. He remembers two "large green French portfolios of colored prints"; a "large library-case" filled with "long rows of old books, that had been printed in Paris, and London, and Leipsic"; and "a fine library edition of the Spectator, in six large volumes with gilded backs"; and "a story-book about Captain Kidd's ship, that lay somewhere at the bottom of the Hudson near the Highlands, full of gold as it could be" (*R* 6–8). He remembers seeing his father's books, but he remembers *reading* the chapbook. His father's books stay in his memory for their material qualities: their fine bindings, gilt tooling, and engraved, hand-colored plates. He had opened the volumes far enough to notice their imprints from faraway places and to look at their pictures, yet he has no recollection of reading them. He may have never read past the title page. He remembers the children's storybook not for its material quality but for its narrative value. His father's books impress him with the notion of old-world culture they represent, while the cheap storybook gives him ideas of adventure and quick, easy wealth. Taken together, fine books and cheap adventure books motivate him to go down to the sea.

Away from home and aboard the *Highlander,* Redburn by no means leaves behind book culture. Much of Melville's description of books and reading aboard ship occurs in Chapter 18, "He Endeavors to Improve His Mind; and Tells of One Blunt and His Dream-Book." The New York friend who had seen Redburn off had given him a volume to take with him. Other sailors had books as well. The man who had killed himself early in the voyage, presumably because of a combination of fear and the DTs, had owned two books, "an account of Shipwrecks and Disasters at Sea" and a volume with the spine title *Delirium Tremens.* The title provides after-the-fact confirmation of the man's self-destructive behavior.

Up to this point in the story, none of Melville's book descriptions seem especially fanciful, yet the last book he describes as "a large black volume, with *Delirium Tremens* in great gilt letters on the back. This proved to be a popular treatise on the subject of that disease; and I remembered seeing several copies in the sailor book-stalls about Fulton Market, and along South-street, in New York" (*R* 86). Melville's physical description is ironic, for sailors hardly patronized the book-stalls in Fulton Market to purchase volumes finely bound and gilt, as a passage from *White-Jacket* clarifies: "Several other sailors were diligent readers, though their studies did not lie in the way of belles-lettres. Their favorite authors were such as you may find at the book-stalls around Fulton Market; they were slightly physiological in their nature" (*WJ* 169). By "slightly physiological" books, Melville meant works such as *Aristotle's Masterpiece,* an illustrated midwifery chapbook often read by men as pornography.[12] Any book about the DTs found at these sailor bookstalls during the 1830s also would have been a chapbook. There were several works titled *Delirium Tremens* available, but all were cheap pamphlets, not weighty tomes.[13] Contemporary readers well knew that a person did not go to the sailor book-stalls to locate quality books. Ironically describing a chapbook as such, Melville blurred the boundaries between popular literature and elite book culture.

Having read the dead man's books, Redburn next prepares to read the book his New York friend had given him. Before doing so, he recalls the gift. His friend had pulled the volume down from a dusty shelf and highly recommended that Redburn read it cover to cover in order to realize its "hidden charms and unforeseen attractions"; he also suggested that Redburn could use the book to help recoup his family's long-exhausted fortune. Taking possession of the book, Redburn had blown the dust from it, glanced first at its spine and then at the title page, felt pleased with the gift as he saw its faraway Aberdeen imprint, and thanked his friend kindly (*R* 86). In a way, the recollected episode, perhaps unnecessarily, duplicates Redburn's boyhood experiences among his father's books. Here again he expresses his fascination with bindings and title pages though he has little notion of the volume's contents.

The book turns out to be Adam Smith's *Wealth of Nations,* a work which had a reputation as "the *Koran* of the modern economists."[14] Before attempting to read it, Redburn imagines the "body of the book" to be "something like the philosopher's stone, a secret talisman, which would transmute even pitch and tar to silver and gold" (*R* 86). Describing the book as a talisman, Redburn anticipates John Paul Jones's description of Benjamin Franklin's *Way to Wealth* as a charm in *Israel Potter.* The friend who gave the Smith volume to Redburn had recommended it as a way to wealth. With great hope, Redburn begins reading its text only to find it as dry "as crackers and cheese," so dry that its "very leaves smelt of saw-dust," so dry that he abandons all hope of reading it. He compares it to his family's "old backgammon board . . . lettered on the back, '*The History of Rome*'" (*R* 87). Redburn's attempt to read Smith's *Wealth of Nations* represents his first attempt to immerse himself in the elite book culture, or more precisely, to move beyond bindings and title pages. His recollection of a gameboard decorated to look like a bound volume, however, suggests that he would rather not enter the elite culture.

He holds on to the volume of Smith but ignores its text, using it only as a material object, for with a jacket wrapped round, it makes a serviceable pillow. As Redburn observes, however, there was one drawback: "I sometimes waked up feeling dull and stupid; but of course the book could not have been the cause of that" (*R* 87). Redburn denies that the book could have any effect on his mind, but Melville, writing "of course the book could not," obviously implied that "of course it could." The passage recalls the schoolboy superstition which stipulates that sleeping with a textbook under the pillow helps the student to learn his lesson.[15] Smith's *Wealth of Nations* can influence Redburn only if it remains closed and unread.

A description of Jack Blunt and his Dream Book takes up the remainder of the chapter. Blunt indulges in all sorts of traditional activities and beliefs. Besides holding numerous superstitions, he sings ballads, tells tales and legends, and practices fortune-telling. One of the stories he tells directly associates superstition and the written word. As the story goes, "a sort of fairy sea-queen . . . used to be dunning a sea-captain all the time for his autograph to boil in some eel soup, for a spell against the scurvy" (*R* 88). According to belief, a person's handwriting served as a powerful talisman, and dissolving a handwritten message and then ingesting the solution was a common superstitious practice.[16] Blunt's story reinforces the link between writing and superstition, a link which Redburn does not seem to understand, for he calls the story incomprehensible.

Since Blunt associates superstition and the written word within his belief system, his ownership of an occult chapbook should come as no surprise. Like most who owned and used (or, I should say, own and use) such works, Blunt keeps his Dream Book well hidden, but he uses it often enough that the other sailors know what it looks like and have a general idea how he uses it. Redburn calls the book an extraordinary looking pamphlet, with a red cover, marked all over with astrological signs and ciphers, and purporting to be a full and complete treatise on the art of Divination; so that the most simple sailor could teach it to himself.

It also purported to be the selfsame system, by aid of which Napoleon Bonaparte had risen in the world from being a corporal to an emperor. Hence it was entitled the *Bonaparte Dream Book*; for the magic of it lay in the interpretation of dreams, and their application to the foreseeing of future events; so that all preparatory measures might be taken beforehand; which would be exceedingly convenient, and satisfactory every way, if true. The problems were to be cast by means of figures, in some perplexed and difficult way, which, however, was facilitated by a set of tables in the end of the pamphlet, something like the Logarithm Tables at the end of Bowditch's Navigator. (*R* 90)

The comparison to Bowditch is significant. First published in the earliest years of the nineteenth century, Bowditch's *Navigator* was recognized almost immediately for its profound improvement over any similar work. Many called it the Sailor's Bible, an epithet which invested it with a power which transcended its numerical tables. Just as Bowditch provided a practical guide to navigate the seas, the Dream Book helped guide a person's way through an uncertain future.

Blunt put great stock in his book's capacity for dream interpretation. As Redburn describes his shipboard behavior, he recalls that Blunt

revered, adored, and worshipped this *Bonaparte Dream Book* of his; and was fully persuaded that between those red covers, and in his own dreams, lay all the secrets of futurity. Every morning before taking his pills, and applying his hair-oils, he would steal out of his bunk before the rest of the watch were awake; take out his pamphlet, and a bit of chalk; and then straddling his chest, begin scratching his oily head to remember his fugitive dreams; marking down strokes on his chest-lid, as if he were casting up his daily accounts. (*R* 90)

After describing how Blunt used the book to discern the ominous meaning of signs which occurred in his dreams, Redburn observes that Blunt's use of the book was all the more remarkable since he could hardly read.

Melville's description of the book is detailed enough to identify precisely the work he means. Furthermore, the description is accurate enough to suggest that on one of his sailor voyages he had witnessed a superstitious sailor using the same work. The chapbook Melville described usually bears the title *Napoleon's Book of Fate*. The original book's text had been purportedly found in an Egyptian tomb. According to legend, Napoleon had consulted the book before every battle.[17] As far as it goes, Melville's description of how to use the book—"cast by means of figures," "marking down strokes," "facilitated by a set of tables in the end of the pamphlet"—is quite accurate. According to the book's directions, the fortune teller had to mark down a random number of vertical strokes in a row. It did not matter how many strokes, as long as the number exceeded twelve, one for each sign of the zodiac. The fortune teller then had to repeat the process four more times, to make a total of five rows of vertical strokes. He then had to count off the first twelve strokes, mark them with a comma, and then count the number of strokes in excess of twelve. If the number of extra strokes were odd, the fortune teller would put one asterisk at the end of the row; if the number of excess strokes were even, then he would place two asterisks at the row's end. The result might look something like this:

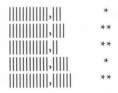

The pattern made by the asterisks would then be applied to a large chart and a series of tables.

The fortune teller would look at the chart, which prefaced the book, and, if he were telling his own fortune, like Blunt, he would ask one of the thirty-two possible questions; if he were telling the fortune of another (something Blunt does not do), he would have that other person ask one of the thirty-two questions. No additional questions were allowed. The supplied questions concerned the basic things anyone interested in foreseeing their future might wish to ask. Some sailors might want to know: "Will my Beloved prove true in my absence?" (Not all sailors' sweethearts were Black-Eyed Susans.)

Someone thinking about entering a big card game might ask: "Shall I make, or mar, my Fortune by Gambling?" Anyone might be interested to know: "Shall I live to an Old Age?" Homesick, seasick, or becalmed sailors might want to know: "Shall I ever recover from my present Misfortunes?" Only one of the thirty-two questions specifically concerned the interpretation of dreams: "Does my Dream portend good luck or misfortune?"

On the chart the questions themselves were aligned along the y-axis (vertical) and the possible patterns of asterisks along the x-axis (horizontal). Within the right angle formed by the axes were what the book calls "hieroglyphic signs"—hand and dagger, hourglass, cornucopia, pyramid, cross-bones, open book, castellated mansion, and shooting star, to name a few. The fortune teller used the index finger of one hand to trace a horizontal line across from the question, and the index finger of the other hand to trace a vertical line from the asterisk-pattern his random vertical strokes had generated. The two lines would meet at a particular hieroglyphic.

The fortune teller would then turn to the tables. Each hieroglyphic corresponded to a table containing thirty-two possible answers; each answer in turn corresponding to a different asterisk pattern. Using the asterisk pattern already generated, the fortune teller would then determine the answer to the question asked.

Since Melville emphasized the book's capacity for dream interpretation, answers to the question, "Does my Dream portend good luck or misfortune?" make good examples. Some possible responses include:

· Thy nightly visions portend good fortune to thee [hieroglyphic of the full moon].
· Thy dream portendeth ill luck to thine enemies [hieroglyphic of the open book].
· It signifieth that thou must take heed to avoid danger [hieroglyphic of the castellated mansion].
· The signification is, that good luck will befall thee [hieroglyphic of the plow].
· It portendeth danger, if thou art not cautious [hieroglyphic of the hand and dagger].
· It importeth, that if thou dost procrastinate, evil will attend thee [hieroglyphic of the moon and stars].

- The signification is *increase of riches* [hieroglyphic of the cross keys].
- It sayeth thou hast enemies who are endeavouring to render thee unhappy [hieroglyphic of the anchor].

In terms of their status, Smith's *Wealth of Nations* and *Napoleon's Book of Fate* switch places during the course of *Redburn:* the elite work takes on superstitious associations, and the chapbook takes on considerable authority. For Wellingborough Redburn, Adam Smith's groundbreaking economic treatise has value only if it remains closed; instead of being a useful guide, Smith's work holds little power beyond the symbolic. In the hands of Jack Blunt, *Napoleon's Book of Fate* becomes a practical conduct book; it acquires its power from being opened and used. Though Blunt could barely read, his possession of the book places him within the literary culture, giving him a status which the unlettered sailors aboard the *Highlander* resent. Passing a wrecked vessel, Blunt observes that "all sailors are saved; they have plenty of squalls here below, but fair weather aloft," whereupon Jackson responds, "And did you get that out of your silly Dream Book, you Greek?" (*R* 104). The tone of Jackson's remark echoes that of the superstitious sailor in *Two Years before the Mast* who resented Richard Henry Dana's Harvard education.[18] For the unlettered, print, even cheap print, remained an object of mystery. To cite another example, when Nehemiah attempts to give the warrior Belex a religious tract in *Clarel,* he spurns it. Djalea must explain Belex's reaction to Nehemiah:

> "The print he likes not; let him be;
> Pray now, he deems it sorcery."
> (*Cl* 2.23.181–82)

MELVILLE CONTRASTED FOLKLORE AND book culture elsewhere in *Redburn.* Wellingborough Redburn carries one volume from the family library with him, a guidebook his father had used in his travels, *The Picture of Liverpool.* He fully intends to use it as a practical guide, but it also serves as a reminder of home and its fine library. Its blank leaves are filled with handwritten notes his father had made about places he went and things he purchased while there. As Redburn attempts to follow its directions upon reaching Liverpool, he realizes the guidebook is much too old to have any lasting practical value. The volume he had treasured "was next to useless. Yes, the thing that had guided the father, could not guide the son" (*R* 157). Instead of tossing it aside as so much wastepaper, however, he retains the volume, and indeed still has it, as he retells the story of his earliest sailor experiences many years later. Without practical value, the book retains symbolic value. Redburn's fondness for the guidebook parallels Blunt's story of the sea queen. Just as the sea queen desires the captain's autograph as an amulet against drowning, Redburn mainly holds on to the volume because it contains his father's (as well as his younger self's) handwriting, a unique feature which gives the volume talismanic power when it no longer has practical value.

Retaining the inscribed book, Redburn anticipates Isabel's behavior in *Pierre*. As she tells Pierre how she first discovered the identity of her father, Isabel explains that she had obtained a handkerchief he had left behind and had noticed his name embroidered in the center. To treasure it all the more, she had laundered and ironed it, folding it "in such a manner, that the name was invisibly buried in the heart of it, and it was like opening a book and turning over many blank leaves before I came to the mysterious writing" (*P* 146). Enfolding the written word within a booklike object enhances its mysterious value. Once in possession of the handkerchief, Isabel begins referring to "Glendinning" as a "talismanic word."

DURING HIS SOJOURN IN Liverpool, Redburn is reminded of another chapbook story for children one Sunday morning. The chime of old church bells in Liverpool, he explains, "carry an admonition with it; something like the premonition conveyed to young Whittington by Bow Bells" (*R* 177). The chapbook story he recalls is *The History of Dick Whittington and His Cat*. Melville had alluded to the work earlier in *Typee*, in which Tommo likens "a big black spectral cat" to "the animal that made the fortune of the ex-lord-mayor Whittington" (*T* 210–11). Melville probably had read the story in his boyhood, for it had appeared in multiple chapbook editions published in Connecticut and New York during his youth.[19]

Referring to the well-known story of Dick Whittington (AT 1651) in *Redburn*, Melville extended his comparison between popular literature and elite book culture to compare a well-known chapbook with the book he was in the process of writing. Both *The History of*

Dick Whittington and His Cat and *Redburn* told stories about poor lads who leave home to seek their livelihoods. Redburn is cruelly abused by Jackson, and Dick Whittington has a cruel abuser in the form of a ruthless cook. Wearied by the cook's cruelty, Whittington runs away. After walking for a time, he sits down to rest, at which point he hears the bow bells that tell him he will become mayor of London some day; he returns to face the cook's ire with the certain knowledge that he will make his way in the world. Here the comparison breaks down, for if Whittington is destined to become Lord-Mayor of London, Redburn will eventually return to New York as poor as when he left.

Blurring the boundaries between elite book culture and the popular book, Melville reflected his own uncertainty toward the idea of authorship. With *Mardi* he had attempted to write a philosophically profound work that would be worthy of the ages yet also would help him to making a living. After that work's commercial failure, Melville set aside his great literary ambitions for the nonce and wrote a work more likely to make money. Not long after completing the book, he wrote to Richard Henry Dana, calling *Redburn* a "little nursery tale of mine" (*Co* 141). The epithet draws a similarity between *Redburn* and such children's stories as *The History of Dick Whittington*, yet it also reflects Melville's frustration with a book that did not fully exploit his rapidly unfolding literary talents. Not long afterwards, he made a similar comment about *Typee* in a letter to Nathaniel Hawthorne, predicting that if his literary fame continued after his death, it would be as the "man who lived among the cannibals" and that children would be given *Typee* "with their gingerbread" (*Co* 193). *Typee*, his most popular work, and *Redburn*, a work he wrote specifically to have greater popular appeal than *Mardi*, Melville associated with the children's chapbook stories. *Mardi*, on the other hand, had a greater affinity to such fine old books as Burton's *Anatomy of Melancholy* and Sir Thomas Browne's *Works*. Though his contrast between the chapbook and elite book culture in *Redburn* challenged the boundaries between the two, it did little to resolve the creative dilemma Melville faced. After completing *Redburn*, he would continue to grapple with the problem: Could a popular story and a philosophically profound work coincide?

SEVEN

Moby-Dick, *Legend*
in the Making

Returning home from London in early 1850, the last bit of distasteful financial business concerning *White-Jacket* behind him,
Herman Melville had to face the task of writing his next book. He
had yet to decide what that book would be, but he was sure of one
thing: he would write the kind of book he wanted to write, a book
unlike either *Redburn* or *White-Jacket,* a book which was not a personal narrative written in haste and overdependent on source material. He continued to think about adapting a chapbook. One he had
known for some time, perhaps since his adolescence, offered the raw
material for a good story: the *Life and Remarkable Adventures of Israel R. Potter... Who Was a Soldier in the American Revolution* (1824).
Melville spent part of his London sojourn thinking about how he
might "serve up" the story of Potter's long exile in Great Britain, and
he absorbed atmosphere and settings useful for retelling it. He even
purchased an old city map that would help him imagine the London
of an earlier generation (*J* 43). Though Potter's story would continue
to intrigue him in the coming years, Melville ultimately decided that
it was not what he wanted to write next.

Rewriting the story of Israel Potter, nonetheless, appealed to
Melville for several reasons, the simplest of which was pragmatic. If
his next book were not to be drawn from his own experience, he
required another source for the basic story. He need not follow the
source closely—his personal narratives, after all, freely embellished
upon his own experiences—but the source would help to give his
book structure during its composition. Once before he had attempted
a book-length fiction not based on personal experience, and that book
had dumbfounded contemporary readers. His experience with *Mardi*
let Melville know that if he were going to write another romance, he
needed a rough outline to follow in order to avoid the philosophical

and speculative morass in which his last ambitious work had become mired during its chartless voyage.

There were numerous other chapbooks he had long known that might have formed the basis for a more substantial narrative. While sightseeing in London, he was reminded of *The History of Dick Whittington and His Cat.* As he recorded the episode, a local fireman guided him through "squalid lanes" to one particular "dirty blind lane," where Whittington's supposed birthplace was marked with a slab (*J* 15). The disappointing marker hardly matched the fond memories of a story Melville had known for years. Though he alluded to Dick Whittington in *Typee* and *Redburn,* Melville expressed no impulse to devote an entire volume to the story. Enormously popular in early America, *The History of Dick Whittington and His Cat* anticipated the Franklinian notions of the American dream, telling of a humbly born young man who makes his rise in the world through diligence and perseverance; yet the work belonged to England's literary history, not America's. Melville's growing devotion to the cause of literary nationalism compelled him to seek an American source.

Most American chapbooks, however, lacked the appeal of the long-standing European ones. First of all, they were not old enough. The story of Dick Whittington went back to the fifteenth century, and chapbooks retelling the story had been in print at least since the seventeenth. Indeed, many of the most widely known European chapbooks had been in print for centuries. The American chapbooks, like the sample of popular literature Taji finds in *Mardi,* were often sensational stories of recent events, frequently concerned with the criminal or the bizarre, hardly the stuff which formed the basis for great literature. Pondering the difficulty American writers faced, Melville asked Evert Duyckinck a rhetorical question: "We may spice up our dishes with all the condiments of the Spice Islands & Moluccas, & our dishes may be all venison & wild boar—yet how the deuce can we make them a century or two old?—My Dear Sir, the two great things yet to be discovered are these—The Art of rejuvenating old age in men, & oldageifying youth in books" (*Co* 127–28). Melville's literary nationalism obliged him to take his material from the New World, yet his sense of what made a good book pulled him toward the Old. The Israel Potter story would allow him to go back several decades, but decades weren't centuries, and Potter, whose life overlapped Melville's by seven years, hardly seemed sufficiently oldageified.

Another problem with American chapbooks was that they lacked supernatural elements or, even more broadly, a sense of wonder. Some of the most memorable European chapbooks, on the other hand, concerned the supernatural. *The History of Dr. Faustus* obviously comes to mind, but there were many others, including *The Famous History of Friar Bacon.* To be sure, some American chapbooks concerned the supernatural, but most of them were akin to Jack Blunt's Dream Book in *Redburn;* in other words, they were prescriptive rather than narrative. They told how to contact the spirit world rather than telling stories of great master-magicians who sought the powers of darkness, imperiling their souls in the process. With growing ambition and an increasingly clear understanding of his own literary abilities, Melville simply wanted what Goethe had had when he sat down to write his great work: a centuries-old story that was part of the national tradition, contained supernatural elements, and had a rich potential for imaginative exploitation. Unable to find the story he wanted within the print culture, Melville returned to his sailor experiences for inspiration. As the narrator in *Mardi* tells himself, "Doctor Faust saw the devil; but you have seen the 'Devil Fish'" (*M* 39). Melville found what he wanted in his memories of the tough yarns he had heard in the forecastle. The sailor's oral tradition brought him to the realm of legend.

Though he had put five books behind him in as many years, Melville had yet to make much creative use of legend. His neglect appears especially obvious in light of the numerous legendary figures, such as Davy Crockett and Mike Fink, who were becoming part of nineteenth-century America's collective personality. Among the most prominent was Sam Patch, a mill hand who had made his reputation (yet ultimately met his fate) leaping down waterfalls. Stories of Sam Patch circulated across America as part of the oral tradition, and chapbook versions were also available.[1] Wellingborough Redburn twice compares himself to the legendary figure. Redburn's earlier allusion to Sam Patch pertains to his own ragtag appearance after wearing landlubber's duds through several days of hard work aboard ship (*R* 75). The second allusion specifically refers to Sam Patch's legendary feats: "For my own part," Redburn, now more experienced, states, "my nerves became as steady as the earth's diameter, and I felt as fearless on the royal yard, as Sam Patch on the cliff of Niagara" (*R* 115). Melville's brief, incidental references do not seem motivated by any particular desire to turn American legend to great art. Indeed, the references may have a more personal than national basis. With the publication of *Typee* he developed a fair reputation as a waterfall jumper himself. Concerning the adventures which Melville described early in *Typee*, George Duyckinck wryly commented in a letter to his brother, "His exploits in descending the waterfalls beat Sam Patch."[2] Melville's published references to Sam Patch may answer private jokes paralleling his life with that of the famous daredevil.

As far as we know, Melville never considered using the legend of Sam Patch for extended literary treatment, though his friend Nathaniel Hawthorne imagined so doing: "How stern a moral may be drawn from the story of poor Sam Patch! Why do we call him a madman or a fool, when he has left his memory around the falls of the Gennessee, more permanently than if the letters of his name had been hewn into the forehead of the precipice?"[3] Hawthorne never wrote the moralized legend of Sam Patch, but his brief comments here say much about the power of traditional stories. The orally circulated legends had become so well known among people living near the waterfall where Sam Patch met his doom that they preserved his memory better than any written record of the man. Oral legend, it seemed, could more effectively perpetuate memory than could the written word. Though Melville may have found intriguing Sam Patch's foolhardy attempts to defy nature by challenging its most awesome power source, Patch was too much an object of humor to justify serious literary treatment. He stood for the worst the New World had to offer, crude sensationalism. To cast Sam Patch as a tragic hero would be bathetic.

As his next book mentally began to take shape, Melville realized that there were other legends far more marvelous and no less American that had much greater literary potential. Any whaleman worth his salt knew the legend of Mocha Dick, the Great White Whale. One contemporary remarked that every "old Jack-tar" was familiar with the story in one form or another.[4] Those who had not heard of Mocha Dick at least had heard of Fightin' Joe, New Zealand Jack, Old Tom, Shy Jack, Spotted Bob, Spotted Tom, Timor Tom, Ugly Tom, or one of the other legendary whales which the Nantucket whaleman had sighted, at least in his mind's eye, since the South Pacific whaling industry had begun.[5]

The various legends share many motifs. Most mention the legendary whale's appearance: not only was it noticeably larger than the average sperm whale (motif B874.3), it had unique coloring or distinguishing marks. In legend, the whale was more often white than any other color, but some legendary whales were dark colored with other unusual features.[6] Spotted Bob, for example, had two large white spots on either side of his head, and New Zealand Tom was "conspicuously distinguished by a white hump."[7] Legendary whales had a terrific range and were often sighted in places far distant from their normal cruising grounds.[8] Many legends tell how the great whale evaded capture. Encountering a legendary whale, much like sighting the Flying Dutchman, brought bad luck.[9] For those who survived, the bad luck could mean anything from stormy weather to poor fishing, but encounters with the legendary whale were often fatal. When pursued by whaleboats, it maliciously turned, attacked, and crushed them in its jaws.[10] Furthermore, it had the power to destroy large sailing vessels.[11] Though there were true stories of vessels being stove by whales, as these stories entered legend they were incorporated with the traditional stories. Through countless retellings, the sinking of the *Essex*, a vessel staved by a whale in the South Pacific in 1820, was ultimately attributed to Mocha Dick.[12] Stories of legendary whales often involved a captain bound and determined to capture the whale. When an old whaling captain begins to tell "a marvelous yarn in relation to the capture of a white whale" in J. Ross Browne's *Etchings of a Whaling Cruise,* for example, he makes it one episode in the life of a legendary captain.[13]

The legends of Mocha Dick and the sinking of the *Essex* provided partial inspiration, yet Melville would synthesize many legends before he finished his new book. Two of the legendary whales he would mention—Morquan, a whale which cruised off the coast of Japan, and Don Miguel, a "Chilean whale, marked like an old tortoise with mystic hieroglyphics upon the back"—are not mentioned in his printed sources.[14] If they are not Melville's own invention, they may reflect legends he had heard in the forecastle during his days as a whaleman. Describing his new book partway through its composition to his English publisher, Richard Bentley, Melville wrote that it was "founded upon certain wild legends in the Southern Sperm Whale Fisheries, and illustrated by the author's own personal experience" (*Co* 163).

Moby-Dick, the name he would settle on for his whale and eventually his book, closely echoes the name of legend's fiercest whale, Mocha Dick, but Melville borrowed elements from multiple stories he had heard from other whalemen. By not calling his whale Mocha Dick, he avoided any one-to-one association with a particular legendary whale. Many have attempted to explain the meaning behind Melville's title. The simplest explanation is that the name incorporates a place name. Several legendary whales received their names from the bodies of land they were associated with, such as New Zealand Jack and Timor Tom. Mocha Dick, after all, was named for Mocha Island off the coast of Chile. The first part of Moby Dick's name may thus refer to a geographic location; like Queequeg's native island, Kokovoko, it is not on any map—but, as Ishmael says, true places never are.

There's little question that Melville strongly believed in the importance of evocative book titles. Disappointed that John Murray retitled *Typee* when that book first appeared in England, Melville expressed great pleasure with Murray's later decision to use Melville's original title for subsequent editions. He wrote Murray, "Rejoiced am I, My Dear Sir, that the magic, cabilistic, *tabooistic* 'Typee' will hereafter grace the title-page of all subsequent English editions of the book" (*Co* 65). The adjectives Melville uses to describe *Typee* seem more appropriate descriptors for Jack Blunt's Dream Book or one of the other occult chapbooks. Though the British edition, which came out first, appeared as *The Whale,* Melville's changed the title to *Moby-Dick* for the American edition—a title that might be similarly described, for it too has cabalistic, tabooistic associations.

Whaling legends gave Melville what the chapbook stories did not. For one thing, they provided him a subject that he could imbue with age. The South Pacific whaling industry had been active for only a few decades, but the story of the whale hunt was not dissimilar to stories which had been around since man could first articulate himself after a hunting expedition. Furthermore, whale-hunting, though a recent commercial venture, used fairly primitive technology compared to other such ventures. At the time Melville wrote *Moby-Dick,* steamers were regularly ferrying passengers across the Atlantic, but the whalers were strictly sailing vessels, and old-fashioned sailing vessels at that. Built for practicality not for speed, the whaling ships lacked the style and grace of the day's magnificent clipper ships.

Weapons, too, were comparatively primitive. Those who hunted land-dwelling creatures had increasingly precise rifles to help them, but mechanical means of accurately propelling a harpoon had yet to surpass the human arm. A whale-hunting story, then, not only brought its readers to the time before steamships, it took them to the time before gunpowder.

The whaling legends could also be considered American national legends. Though set inside that great triangle from Kamchatka to Fiji to Juan Fernández, and peopled with sailors from the Isle of Man to the Society Islands, the whaling industry was an American industry. It had had its start among Native Americans; or, even if it had not, Melville knew that a good enough case could be made for the aboriginal Nantucketers as the earliest whalemen. Furthermore, descendants of European settlers living on Nantucket since the late seventeenth century—the Starbucks, the Coffins, the Swains—had practiced offshore whaling. Whaling ventures were financed by American investors, and whaling ships were built by American shipbuilders and sailed by American captains. The story of a successful whaling voyage confirmed the Franklinian notions of the American dream, as it showed how hard work, sacrifice, and risk taking could result in profit and glory. And it did so on a grandiose scale.

Whaling legends had an added advantage over other contemporary American legends, for they offered a much greater potential for evoking a sense of awe and wonder. Davy Crockett might slay the occasional grizzly with his bare hands, but his efforts seem tame compared to pursuing the leviathan with naught but harpoon and lance. Truthful, unembellished whaling stories were more awe inspiring than even legendary, highly embellished bear stories. Melville described Owen Chase's genuine *Narrative of the Most Extraordinary and Distressing Shipwreck of the Whale-Ship Essex* as a "wondrous story," much the same language he used to describe the fanciful legend of how the Indians settled Nantucket, a "wondrous traditional story" (*MD* 63). The whale's size, power, and capacity for destruction evoked a sense of wonder that no other creature on earth could provide.

Whaling legends also held potential for imaginative supernaturalism. The whale's whiteness, to cite only one of its legendary aspects, allowed for numerous supernatural associations. Eventually these would come together as "The Whiteness of the Whale," but well before Melville had the idea for that chapter, he had recognized the supernatural potential of whiteness. It was a magic color (motif D1293.3). In *Omoo* a piece of white tappa affixed to the flying jib boom is a "mystic symbol" that serves to deter a group of otherwise willing wahines (*O* 20). In *Mardi* the "ghastly White Shark" is a "ghost of a fish" which expresses "horrific serenity" (*M* 41). Few sights prompted a sailor's fear more greatly than white water (motif F711.3.1). When the sea appears "white as a shroud" in *Mardi,* the narrator fears for his life (*M* 123). White was traditionally associated with death, from the pallor of the dead and the color of a ghost (motif E422.4.3). The whitewashed walls of the hospital aboard the *Neversink,* covered with dreary shadows, make it look like "a whited sepulchre under ground" (*WJ* 336). White sea birds, it goes without saying, represented the souls of deceased sailors.

The whaling legend had practical advantages similar to those of a chapbook story, for both supplied a basic story on which Melville could build a greater narrative. Adapting whaling legends had an advantage over chapbook stories for Melville, because he could use his personal experience to enliven the story without having to rely on personal experience for its structure. Legends, combined with his firsthand knowledge of whaling (well supplemented with printed sources), allowed Melville to create a fantastic story which, almost paradoxically, contained much realistic detail. Furthermore, the whaling story would allow him to avoid the excesses of *Mardi*. He could indulge in *Mardi*-esque speculations, but whenever he felt himself delving too deeply into metaphysics, he could stops chasing chimeras and get back to the business of chasing whales.

Having decided to tell the greatest whaling story ever told, Melville set out to accomplish the task. And he did. But how? His debt to English belles lettres is well known—Robert Burton, Sir Thomas Browne, and the King James Bible for prose style; Milton for a sense of epic grandeur; Shakespeare for language, the idea of the tragic hero, and general inspiration—but Melville's debt to oral literature has never been fully acknowledged. Besides borrowing the legend of the great whale as his theme, Melville also borrowed, and enhanced, many legendary motifs. Legend told how the same whale was found in distant parts of the globe. In *Moby-Dick* Melville wrote that one legend that gained currency among the "superstitiously inclined" was that Moby Dick was ubiquitous, "that he had actually been encountered in opposite latitudes at one and the same instant of time" (*MD*

182). The legends emphasized the great whale's ability to avoid capture. Moby Dick is immortal. Knowing "that after repeated, intrepid
assaults, the White Whale had escaped alive," some whalemen went
further, "declaring Moby Dick not only ubiquitous, but immortal
(for immortality is but ubiquity in time)" (*MD* 183). The legendary
whales often took on much greater powers than their real-life coun-
terparts. Rumors of Moby Dick, Ishmael observes, compounded with
"all manner of morbid hints, and half-formed foetal suggestions of
supernatural agencies," gave it "new terrors unborrowed from anything that visibly appears" (*MD* 181).

Melville articulated the story of a legendary whale better than even
the best forecastle yarn spinner, yet it may be unfair to equate Melville's
task of writing with an old salt's storytelling. Melville's novel has an
audience different from that of the whaleman's legend. In the forecastle, the storyteller and his audience are all whalemen. Together
they share a knowledge of the genuine dangers involved with whale
hunting, the fear which comes from that knowledge, and the belief
in numerous superstitions which help them cope with their hazard-
ous pursuit. Of all sailors, Melville wrote, whalemen "are by all odds
the most directly brought into contact with whatever is appallingly
astonishing in the sea; face to face they not only eye its greatest marvels, but, hand to jaw, give battle to them" (*MD* 180). Their firsthand
experience with whales combined with their folk beliefs made a gath-
ering of whalemen an ideal audience for fantastic whaling legends.

Meville's storyteller, one Ishmael, though an experienced
whaleman, differs greatly from the forecastle storytellers. Ishmael is a
bookman. As he proudly states, "I have swam through libraries and
sailed through oceans" (*MD* 136). He owns a good collection of books
himself and uses dried bits of whaleskin for bookmarks. Witty and
urbane, he can hold his own in conversation among fine Spanish
cavaliers upon the thick-gilt, tiled piazza of the Golden Inn at Lima.
By his own assertion, he is not superstitious, yet he clearly has mastered the tall tale. Melville's intended readers, too, differ greatly from
the superstitious whalemen. They know their Shakespeare and their
Milton, and at least the best of them have read Burton and Browne.
They know virtually nothing about the whaling industry save for the
fact that when day turns to night and they must light a lamp to continue their studies into the evening, they owe a debt of gratitude to
the intrepid whaleman. They are not superstitious, or at least not

much. Though more at home with pipe and snifter than chaw and flask, Melville's intended readers still needed a certain mental toughness. Melville cautioned Sarah Morewood against reading *Moby-Dick,* telling her, "Warn all gentle fastidious people from so much as peeping into the book—on risk of a lumbago & sciatics" (*Co* 206). One of the biggest challenges Melville faced was to retell a folk legend for those who were not whalemen—in other words, who did not belong to the folk group to which the legend belonged.

Legend theorists generally agree that legends derive their believability from the realism of their everyday detail and from the underlying folk beliefs of those who tell and hear them.[15] To bring a whaling legend to his readers, Melville had to provide enough background detail for them to understand the daily reality of the whaleman, and he also had to detail their folk beliefs. Though some modern readers find the numerous whaling chapters cumbersome and would prefer to reach the cetological center as quickly as possible, these chapters are essential. Only by providing such information could Melville viably recreate a whaling legend for bourgeois landlubbers.

Some chapters describe the process of whaling to help convince readers that the story, fantastic though it may seem, was possible. The navigational detail set forth in "The Chart" suggests the possibility of encountering the same whale a second time. "The Affidavit" provides empirical testimony that whales could indeed destroy large vessels. Several of the chapters specifically concern the whaleman's working life. "The First Lowering," "The Line," "Cutting In," "The Monkey Rope," and "The Try-Works," just to name a few, help give readers a good sense of the difficult work involved hunting the whale. The remarks of prominent twentieth-century watercolorist Charles Burchfield provide one indication that Melville recreated the whaleman's workaday life well. Reading one of Melville's whaling chapters, Burchfield commented, "The description of the end of the day after a hard day of chasing whales. Must a man after all be a hard physical worker to enjoy the world[?] It would seem so."[16] Melville's description of the whole process comes to a close with Chapter 98, "Stowing Down and Clearing Up."

The following chapter, "The Doubloon," marks a key turning point in *Moby-Dick*. Coming immediately after the final chapter describing the whaling process, it marks a withdrawal from the natural, realistic world and a total immersion in the supernatural. Ahab had first nailed the doubloon to the mast back in Chapter 36, "The Quarter-Deck," but it had not been mentioned since. "The Doubloon" serves to refocus the narrative, bringing all the principal characters together and reminding them of their quest. The chapter's careful structure also draws readers away from their comfortable world of books and into the world of superstition and folk belief.

Before anyone approaches the doubloon, Ishmael explains the crew's general attitude toward the coin. They revere it "as the white whale's talisman," wonder who will get it, and "whether he would ever live to spend it" (*MD* 431). Making the doubloon Moby Dick's talisman, Melville reversed traditional sailor superstitions about coins. Shipbuilders often put a coin where the mast was stepped into the kelson as a lucky charm; it assured fishing boats prosperity and protected oceangoing vessels from harm. The *Constitution*, for example, had coins under each mast.[17] Another superstition allowed the captain of a sailing vessel to use a coin to buy wind from the devil. As in whistling for a wind, however, the captain who tried to buy wind often got more than he bargained for. One old salt explained, "I have seen captains throw a quarter or fifty cents overboard, saying, 'Give me that much of wind.' Sometimes they get too much when they buy it."[18] The doubloon, like the coin used to buy wind, seems a way to recruit the devil's powers in order to fulfill the captain's desire. Nailed to the mast, the doubloon occupies the place of a ship's traditional talisman, the lucky horseshoe. As the chapter unfolds, we learn that the *Pequod* has a horseshoe nailed to the mast directly opposite the doubloon, but when the chapter begins, that fact has yet to be revealed. Instead, it seems as if the *Pequod* carries Moby Dick's talisman precisely where it should be carrying its own. When the Old Manxman recognizes the juxtaposition of doubloon and horseshoe later in the chapter, he prophesies doom for the *Pequod*.

One after another, all the book's principal characters except Ishmael approach the doubloon and offer their interpretations. Some recognize its superstitious implications, while others do not. Stubb is the third to approach. Like Ishmael, Stubb had watched Ahab and Starbuck and listened to their interpretations. Ahab had seen himself in the coin and used the proverbial comparison "as proud as Lucifer" to describe the appearance of the three tall peaks depicted on the doubloon. Starbuck had seen the coin's iconography in traditional Christian terms. After Stubb has his say, he finds a comfortable hiding place from which to watch the crew members who follow. Stubb thus takes over the narration from Ishmael, though the takeover is not made explicit; Stubb's narrative is embedded within Ishmael's. Taken literally, Ishmael abandons his own voice and becomes Stubb's amanuensis. As a surrogate narrator, Stubb parallels Ishmael. He represents a kind of halfway point between the unsuperstitious, well read, and articulate Ishmael and the unlettered, superstitious sailors. Stubb's interpretation of the doubloon's iconography and his subsequent narration place him between the oral culture and the written word.

Stubb mentions five books: Bowditch's *Navigator,* Nathan Daboll's *Arithmetic,* the *Massachusetts Calendar,* James Ferguson's *Astronomy,* and Lindley Murray's *English Grammar.* Stubb's bookish references clearly reveal his level of education. He knows the day's most important school textbooks in arithmetic and grammar; he is a good enough seaman to have dipped into Bowditch, though he apparently does not own a copy. His modest book learning has given him the confidence to belittle others who possess even smaller amounts of book knowledge, such as "the old women [who] talk Ferguson's Astronomy in the back country" (*MD* 434).[19]

When Stubb draws on his scholarly knowledge to interpret the doubloon's iconography, however, he reveals its inadequacy. The zodiacal signs on the coin remind him of other places where he had seen the same signs: "That, now is what old Bowditch in his Epitome calls the zodiac, and what my almanack below calls ditto. I'll get the almanack; and as I have heard devils can be raised with Daboll's arithmetic, I'll try my hand at raising a meaning out of these queer curvicues here with the Massachusetts calendar" (*MD* 432). Stubb hardly seems to differentiate between the three books he mentions. Bowditch's work had a reputation for astronomical and scientific precision, while the almanac was a repository of age-old astrological lore; since both contain pictures of the zodiac, however, Stubb finds them interchangeable. Daboll's work, like Bowditch's, had developed an authoritative reputation. Like other books of great authority, Daboll's work had taken on legendary powers that transcended its text. In Melville's day, the phrase "according to Daboll" had become proverbial.[20] That Stubb largely equates all three books suggests that any printed object bound and gathered into leaves held the potential for supernatural power.

Stubb tries to use his *Massachusetts Calendar* to interpret the doubloon, but he has difficulty, exclaiming, "Book! you lie there; the fact is, you books must know your places. You'll do to give us the bare words and facts, but we come in to supply the thoughts. That's my small experience, so far as the Massachusetts calendar, and Bowditch's navigator, and Daboll's arithmetic go" (*MD* 433). Stubb's initial acceptance of the book as a conduit to the supernatural and his subsequent recognition of it as something containing just "bare words and facts" show him oscillating between folk belief and literary culture.

Another crew member has also been watching the others approach the doubloon: Pip. When his turn comes, he states, "I look, you look, he looks; we look, ye look, they look." Characteristically, Stubb uses his book learning to try to understand Pip's comment: "Upon my soul, he's been studying Murray's Grammar" (*MD* 434). Pip did not know Murray; he had no training in verb conjugation. Pip is simply commenting on what he saw. As Pip continues to speak, his seemingly crazy comments defy Stubb's interpretive efforts and discomfort him to such an extent that he abandons his observations and therefore relinquishes his role as narrator. Significantly, Ishmael's voice does not return to close the chapter; rather, Pip gets the last word. Unlike Stubb's, Pip's comments are not narrative. Set inside quotation marks, they occur as direct discourse, and appropriately, for Pip's remarks come exclusively from the oral culture, combining folktale, superstition, personal legend, proverb, and song. Pip says: "Here's the ship's navel, this doubloon here, and they are all on fire to unscrew it. But, unscrew your navel, and what's the consequence?" Pip does not answer the question, but the answer, according to a humorous folk belief, is that when you unscrew your navel, your backside falls off. The idea may allude to a folktale. In *V*, Thomas Pynchon would retell a story of a boy born with a golden screw where his navel should have been.[21] Pynchon's story echoes a traditional tale, but it also pays homage to Melville.

Pip follows his question with an omen: he explains, "When aught's nailed to the mast it's a sign that things grow desperate." He then briefly relates a personal legend describing a parallel event: "My father, in old Tolland county, cut down a pine tree once, and found a silver ring grown over in it; some old darkey's wedding ring." Then comes a proverbial phrase: "God goes 'mong the worlds blackberrying." Pip closes the chapter with a snatch from the minstrel song, "Old King Crow":

> Cook! ho, cook! and cook us! Jenny! hey, hey, hey, hey, hey, Jenny, Jenny! and get your hoe-cake done!
> (*MD* 435)

In "The Doubloon" Pip finishes what Stubb had started. Stubb had begun the transition from Ishmael's world of books to the sailor's world of folk belief and superstition, and Pip completes it, taking the reader outside the realm of written culture, back to a preliterate, nonrational, intuitive, instinctive world.

After "The Doubloon," the superstitions become more and still more numerous as the final chase nears. Back in Chapter 41, "Moby Dick," Ishmael had explained that the whaleman's detachment from "any chiselled hearthstone, or aught hospitable beneath that part of the sun" provided sufficient isolation to let his superstitious belief flourish and therefore to give credence to seemingly fantastic, supernatural legends (*MD* 180). Writing for a civilized audience, people who sat near chiseled hearthstones as they read, Melville had to recapture the whaleman's sense of isolation from all things civilized. To immerse his readers completely in the fantastic world of whaling legends, Melville realized, he had to overwhelm them with charms, conjurations, and mighty magic.

By no means was it an impossible task. Even if his readers were not superstitious, they were not so detached from folk belief that they could not indulge themselves with superstitions occasionally. During the Thanksgiving holiday in 1850, after Melville had committed himself to writing *Moby-Dick*, family members gathered at Arrowhead, his Pittsfield home, for festivities. One evening they diverted themselves with Caroline Howard Gilman's *Oracles from the Poets: A Fanciful Diversion for the Drawing-Room.*[22] Gilman's work, popularly known as "Home Oracles," presents a series of questions, each with several possible answers in the form of poetical quotations. The book, which had gone through several editions since first appearing in 1844, was a sort of bourgeois version of Jack Blunt's Dream Book. Such parlor prophesizing would have shown Melville that the difference between home oracles and sea oracles was a difference in degree and not in kind. Recasting sailor superstitions within an ambitious literary work, Melville brought the whaleman's world of superstitious belief to his stay-at-home readers—or so he hoped. Only the best contemporary readers, however, recognized the importance of superstitions to *Moby-Dick*. Reviewing *The Whale*, G. H. Lewes, for example, commented, "Ordinary superstitions related by vulgar pens have lost their power over all but the credulous; but Imagination has a credulity of its own respondent to power. So it is with Melville's superstitions: we believe in them imaginatively."[23]

Many of the superstitions that arise late in the book directly concern Ahab. Though aware of the numerous omens revealed to him, Ahab expresses ambivalence toward them. He instructs his men not to believe in superstitions, yet he himself cannot resist. During the first day of the final chase, Ahab's whale boat is stove. Its shattered planks are retrieved and set on the *Pequod*'s deck, and Starbuck calls the broken boat "an omen, and an ill one." Ahab responds, "Omen? omen?—the dictionary! If the gods think to speak outright to man, they will honorably speak outright; not shake their heads, and give an old wives' darkling hint" (*MD* 553). After the second day of the final chase, however, Ahab does an about-face and encourages his men's superstitious belief. He tells them, "Believe ye, men, in the things called omens? Then laugh aloud, and cry encore! For ere they drown, drowning things will twice rise to the surface; then rise again, to sink for evermore." Ahab immediately realizes that he has just contradicted what he had told them the day before. He mutters to himself, "The things called omens! And yesterday I talked the same to Starbuck there, concerning my broken boat. Oh! how valiantly I seek to drive out of others' hearts what's clinched so fast in mine!" (*MD* 562).

Long before the second day of the final chase, however, Ahab had revealed his superstitious predilections. Visiting Perth the blacksmith in "The Forge," Ahab sees the sparks flying about the anvil as the blacksmith works and asks him, "Are these thy Mother Carey's chickens, Perth? they are always flying in thy wake; birds of good omen, too, but not to all;—look here, they burn; but thou—thou liv'st among them without a scorch" (*MD* 487). Ahab calls the sight of Mother Carey's chickens a good omen but acknowledges that they did not mean good luck for everyone. According to folk belief, the bird is more often considered a bad omen. Its other name, the stormy petrel, emphasizes its association with bad weather.[24] Melville himself provided fuller explanations of the bird's superstitious import in later writings. In "The Encantadas," the stormy petrel's "chirrup under the stern is ominous to mariners as to the peasant the death-tick sounding from behind the chimney jam" (*PT* 136). In *Clarel* Melville used the image of the Mother Carey's chicken as an epic simile. Describing how Rolfe appears deep within a ravine, the narrator explains:

> Far down see Rolfe there, hidden low
> By ledges slant. Small does he show
> (If eagles eye), small and far off
> As Mother Cary's bird in den
> Of Cape Horn's hollowing billow-trough,
> When from the rail where lashed they bide
> The sweep of overcurling tide,—
> Down, down, in bonds the seamen gaze
> Upon that flutterer in glen
> Of waters where it sheltered plays,
> While, over it, each briny hight
> Is torn with bubbling torrents white
> In slant foam tumbling from the snow
> Upon the crest; and far as eye
> Can range through mist and scud which fly,
> Peak behind peak the liquid summits grow.
> (*Cl* 3.29.8–23)

Melville's imagery here shows the stormy petrel's paradoxical role. The rough seas and towering waves that imperil the sailor serve as shelter for the bird.

Ahab, carrying a "small rusty-looking leathern bag," visits the blacksmith with a specific purpose. Showing the bag's contents to Perth, Ahab tells him, "Look ye, blacksmith, these are the gathered nail-stubs of the steel shoes of racing horses." The blacksmith's description of the horseshoe stubs is utilitarian—"the best and stubbornest stuff we blacksmiths ever work." Ahab, on the other hand, uses a colorful simile to describe the forged results: "I know it old man; these stubs will weld together like glue from the melted bones of murderers" (*MD* 488). What neither says is that iron had traditional magic associations (motif D1252.1.1), and horseshoe stubs, like horseshoes, had supernatural powers (motif G224.13.1). One British legend tells of a witch who shook and rattled a bottle of horse-nail stumps in front of a person she meant to bewitch.[25] Ahab's newly forged iron soon takes on further supernatural powers in "The Candles" as it becomes engulfed in the mysterious light of the corposants.

The harpoon iron, like his vial of Nantucket soundings, becomes another personal talisman for Ahab. After his boat is stove the first day of the chase, he asks Stubb about the harpoon's safety before he inquires about that of his men. One depended on the other, though: the harpoon gives Ahab a way to control his men and guide them to his purpose. It functions as an object of homeopathic magic, for just as the horse-nail stumps are welded together to Ahab's end, so too are his men: "They were one man, not thirty ... all the individualities of the crew, this man's valor, that man's fear; guilt and guiltlessness, all varieties were welded into oneness, and were all directed to that fatal goal which Ahab their one lord and keel did point to" (*MD* 557).

Surveying the more extensive damage at the end of the second day of the chase, Ahab realizes that Fedallah has disappeared. Stubb tells him that he thought he had seen Fedallah caught among the tangles of his line, a piece of information Ahab receives with panic, for Fedallah's death would fulfill the first half of the prophecy of his own death: "*My* line! *my* line? Gone?—gone? What means that little word?—What death-knell rings in it, that old Ahab shakes as if he were the belfry. The harpoon, too!—toss over the litter there,—d'ye see it?—the forged iron, men, the white whale's—no, no, no,—blistered fool! this hand did dart it!—'tis in the fish!" (*MD* 561).

Ahab's whalebone leg had also been splintered during the encounter, so he has the carpenter make him a new leg. Earlier, Ishmael had explained that Ahab kept several spare whalebone legs aboard, so the carpenter's work seems an unnecessary duplication; yet this new leg differs significantly from his spare ones, for Ahab has the carpenter make it from the broken keel of the wrecked whaling boat. The new leg thus takes on great symbolic power, and it too functions as a talisman. Since his specially forged harpoon is now lodged in Moby Dick's flesh, Ahab needs a new amulet. Made from his whaling boat's keel, Ahab's new leg recalls the canes made from the *Constitution*'s timbers that Melville had mentioned elsewhere. The new prosthetic is also an object of homeopathic magic: just as Ahab is "one lord and keel" to his crew, he himself is now supported by a keel. The new leg has further significance in that it is made from wood that had been touched by Moby Dick. Thus it also possesses contagious magic: since Moby Dick had touched the whaleboat, its wood shares the great whale's magical powers. In making a leg from a boat shattered by the great whale, however, Ahab offers yet another act of defiance. It would be his last.

In "The Chase—Third Day," Ishmael explains the fate of Ahab's harpoon; it is among the fresh irons corroding in Moby Dick that madden the beast to such an extent that he seems "possessed by all the angels that fell from heaven" (*MD* 567). Like the doubloon, Ahab's harpoon has become Moby Dick's talisman. Now in possession of the harpoon, Moby Dick gains its supernatural power and uses it to destroy Ahab.

Melville's strategy of piling superstitions on superstitions in order to draw his readers into the whaleman's legendary world ultimately proved effective. The book was too daring and innovative to gain wide acceptance initially, yet some contemporary readers appreciated Melville's use of superstition. The reviewer for the London *Atlas* likened reading *The Whale* to being under "the spell of a magician who works wildly, recklessly, but with a skill and a potency which few, we should think, will be disposed either to deny or resist."[26] When *Moby-Dick* began to be reread after decades of neglect, others fell under Melville's magic spell. Robert Buchanan, an important early figure in the Melville revival, called Melville a "sea-magician."[27] Though few who read *Moby-Dick* could articulate precisely what drew them to it, many could not help but admit that the book left them spellbound.

EIGHT

Legend, Belief, Tradition, and Clarel

Herman Melville's extended vacation to Europe, the Mediterranean, and the Holy Land from late 1856 through early 1857 gave him much to occupy his thought and his pen through the remainder of his life. His visit to Italy inspired many of his late poems, and his time in Jerusalem and its environs gave him the experience that eventually led to *Clarel, A Poem and Pilgrimage in the Holy Land*. Though the kernel of Melville's great poem is apparent in his trip journal— he rails against "the great curse of modern travel—skepticism," for example (*J* 97)—*Clarel* was then still many years away. More immediately, the vacation provided ideas he could use during his career as a lecturer. Sightseeing experiences gave him the topic for "Statuary in Rome," which he presented several times around the United States during the first lecture season after he returned home. Melville's initial foray into lecturing was not entirely successful, however. The next winter he returned to a more tried-and-true subject, "The South Seas." Though better received than the "Statuary" lecture, "The South Seas" was not as successful as it could have been, for Melville staunchly refused to give audiences what they wanted. While numerous testimonies document Melville's oral tale-telling ability, he would not draw the long bow and play the folk hero in his lectures.[1] Instead, he assumed an understated, scholarly pose. Tommo had turned professor.

The parallel between Greece and the South Pacific had occurred to Melville as he sailed through the Mediterranean, and he reiterated it in the South Seas lecture. He saw the modern-day Greek isles as a sort of debauched Polynesia. The Polynesian isles were as "fresh as at their first creation," but the Greek ones had "lost their virginity" and looked worn and meager, "like life after enthusiasm is gone" (*J* 72). Primitive Polynesia, in other words, provided an analogue for ancient Greece. In the South Seas lecture Melville paralleled a Polynesian legend with Greek mythology, vaguely mentioning one legend which had "much of the grace, strangeness, and audacity of the Grecian fables" (*PT* 418–19). Though Melville did not name the story in the lecture, newly discovered evidence shows that he was referring to the Hawaiian legend of Umi.[2] Before writing the lecture, he had borrowed from his friend Gorham Dummer Gilman, a longtime Hawaiian resident, a manuscript journal that retold the Umi story, among other Hawaiian legends. Upon returning it, Melville reiterated his enthusiasm in a letter to Gilman: "Your Journal was very interesting to me,—the tale of Umi exceedingly so. I was charmed with it. It is graceful & Greekish" (*Co* 380). In the same letter Melville admitted to his friend that he had tried adapting the tale but, dissatisfied with the results, had abandoned the attempt.

The legend which Gilman recorded and Melville attempted to rewrite tells how Liloa, a great Hawaiian chief, encountered the beautiful Akahaikuleana during a long excursion away from his chiefdom. After spending much time together, they realized she was pregnant. Liloa, who had to return to the island of Hawaii, gave Akahaikuleana tokens of his time with her and told her to name the child Umi if a boy. The child indeed turned out to be a boy, and some years later his mother gave Umi the same tokens to bring to his father. Upon receiving them and learning the boy's name, Liloa welcomed Umi and treated him as his son, much to the chagrin of Hakau, Liloa's legitimate son. After Liloa's death, Hakau became the Hawaiian king and proved to be both cruel and irresponsible. Umi then murdered his half-brother and became a wise and just king.

In comparing the Hawaiian legend to a Grecian fable in the "South Seas" lecture and labeling it "Greekish" in his letter to Gilman, Melville clearly recognized its similarity to traditional Greek stories. As a fratricide, it recalls the story of Eteocles and Polynices, both sons of Oedipus. At their father's death, the two brothers agreed to share the crown, reigning in alternate years. Eteocles served first, but when his year was up he refused to relinquish the throne to his brother. Polynices then left Thebes for Argos, returning with a formidable army led by seven famous generals. In turn, Eteocles established formidable defenses guarding each of the seven gates of Thebes. After much bloodshed on both sides, the two brothers agreed to settle the dispute by single combat, during which they both fell.

Melville himself had told a similar story in *Mardi*. On the island of Juam there reigned a king called Teei, but his succession had been long disputed by his brother Marjora. Eventually Marjora defeated Teei and sent him fleeing for his life. Teei fled to Willamilla, where Marjora pursued and ferociously killed him, stripped from his body the royal girdle, wound it round his own loins, and proclaimed himself king of Juam. The island accepted his sovereignty, but eventually a sacred oracle declared that since Marjora had slain his brother Teei in Willamilla, where his body would remain for eternity, Marjora could not leave Willamilla, nor could any of his descendants who succeeded to the throne. The king of Juam must lodge forever in Willamilla (*M* 220–21).

Melville's refusal to capitalize in his lecture on his personal experiences in the South Pacific does not mean that he was unwilling to reuse the South Pacific's oral tradition in his writings. His attempt to rework the Umi legend, a story that paralleled the story of the kings in Willamilla, suggests that he was not averse to using material similar to what he had used before. The parallel he made between the Umi legend and Greek mythology reflects his newfound interest in ancient culture. A visitor to Arrowhead, in a literary pilgrimage the month after Melville had finished his second lecture season, found him "soured by criticism and disgusted with the civilized world. . . . The ancient dignity of Homeric times afforded the only state of humanity, individual or social, to which he could turn with any complacency."[3] Taken together, the similarities among the Umi legend, Greek myth, and the *Mardi* episode suggest that the Umi story provided Melville a way to connect his personal experience in the South Pacific with ancient Greece.

Melville's journey to the Holy Land gave him experience that ultimately allowed him to appreciate Christian legend as he had the primitive legends of Polynesia and Greece. Before the journey he had never fully appreciated Christian legends because he had been unable to distance himself from them. In the Marquesas he had seen mankind in a simple, natural state, and his Marquesan experience allowed him to imagine ancient Greece similarly. He obviously could not view Christianity as part of a simpler past, for the Christian era continued into the present. People who held Christian beliefs had been partially responsible for the downturn in Polynesian culture and, for that matter, for upholding a conservative morality that doomed the forward-thinking aesthetic innovations which Melville's finest work embodied. His personal animosity toward Christianity made it difficult for him to approach Christian legend with objectivity. Furthermore, religious doubts continued to trouble him. Questioning his faith in Christianity, Melville could scarcely appreciate legends which exemplified such faith. Since his personal belief system did not factor into his understanding of South Pacific legends or Greek mythology, he could more easily appreciate them for their aesthetic qualities.

Melville's religious doubts accompanied him to Europe in 1856. Shortly after arriving in Great Britain, he stopped at Liverpool to visit his old friend Nathaniel Hawthorne, who recorded the gist of their conversations. Hawthorne's notebook entries well reflect his friend's state of mind: "Melville, as he always does, began to reason of Providence and futurity, and of everything that lies beyond human ken.... He can neither believe, nor be comfortable in his unbelief; and he is too honest and courageous not to try to do one or the other."[4] Some years earlier Melville had looked to Sir Thomas Browne's belief system as a model. In *Mardi* Taji states, "Be Sir Thomas Brown our ensample; who, while exploding 'Vulgar Errors,' heartily hugged all the mysteries in the Pentateuch" (*M* 39). As Melville interpreted him, Browne saw no contradiction between blasting superstition while believing all the wonders associated with Christianity. Though Melville may have admired Browne's acceptance of the Christian faith, he could not emulate it. His trip to the Holy Land by no means reconciled his religious doubts, but it greatly enriched his understanding of and relationship to Christianity.

As the "storied weapons" mounted in the entry of the Spouter-Inn help make fantastic whaling legends more tangible for Ishmael in *Moby-Dick*, Melville's contact with the material objects and physical places associated with Christian legends gave them tangibility and ultimately allowed him to recognize how he could make literary use of Christian legend. Almost two decades passed between the time Melville returned from Jerusalem and the publication of *Clarel*, however; his assimilation of the experience obviously required much effort. Besides recognizing how to adapt his own journey to the Holy Land as a fictional narrative, Melville also had to make the difficult decision to tell the lengthy narrative in verse. And before he could even consider writing a long narrative poem, he had to train himself as a poet.[5]

Melville took an important step toward synthesizing Christian legend and narrative verse when he acquired a copy of Francis James

Child's eight-volume *English and Scottish Ballads* during the late 1850s.[6] In addition, the work provided continuity between his current interests and his experience as a sailor. Included within Child's work were two salt-sea ballads that the fictional Jack Chase sings aboard the *Neversink* in *White-Jacket* and that the real-life Jack Chase presumably sang aboard the *United States,* "Sir Patrick Spens" and "The Mermaid." Reading the ballads would have brought back fond memories of his Navy friend, but they would also have reinforced the literary importance of traditional ballads, something Jack Chase had impressed upon him long ago. Think of it: here were some of the same ballads Melville had heard among unlettered sailors, prefaced with scholarly introductions, annotated, and appended with variants. Ned Ballad's red flannel had given way to boiled shirts and kid gloves.

Not all the volumes survive, but those that do contain brief notes Melville made as he read them. Some of the marked portions anticipate passages in *Clarel*. Melville scored several lines in "The Wandering Jew," a ballad that retells a legend Melville himself would retell as "The Masque" (bk. 3, canto 19).[7] He also scored the following passage in Child's introduction to "Hugh of Lincoln": "The exquisite tale which Chaucer has put into the mouth of the prioress exhibits nearly the same incidents as the following ballad. The legend of Hugh of Lincoln was widely famous."[8] Both "The Prioress's Tale" and the ballad told the legend of Hugh of Lincoln, a boy who accidentally kicked a ball through the window of a Jew's home and met his gruesome demise at the hands of the Jew's daughter, who had lured him inside:

> She's led him in through ae dark door,
> And sae has she thro nine;
> She's laid him on a dressing-table,
> And stickit him like a swine.
>
> And first came out the thick, thick, blood,
> And syne came out the thin,
> And syne came out the bonny heart's blood;
> There was nae mair within.

In *Clarel* Ungar says that "Old ballads sing / Fair Christian children crucified / By impious Jews" and specifically refers to Hugh of Lincoln (4.9.129–31). The reference does more than simply pay homage to an important source of inspiration: it gives the ballad an ongoing relevance, as it provides an analogue for the explanation of children in modern-day factories. Ungar continues his diatribe and queries:

> How many Hughs of Lincoln, say,
> Does Mammon in his mills, to-day,
> Crook, if he do not crucify?
> (4.9.133–35)

Child's association between the traditional ballad and Chaucer's *Canterbury Tales* clearly attracted Melville's attention. Casting his own narrative of a pilgrimage in verse, Melville recognized a similarity between his work and Chaucer's, yet he saw the profound differences between a medieval pilgrimage and a modern one—nineteenth-century pilgrims hardly shared the unwavering faith of their predecessors. Clarel's doubts are apparent from his first speech in Book I. As the pilgrimage begins in Book II, the narrator makes an explicit comparison to Chaucer's Canterbury pilgrims yet lets his readers know that conditions have changed significantly since Chaucer's time: "Another age, and other men, / And life an unfulfilled romance" (2.1.12–13). Brief and simple, these lines convey the impossibility of recapturing medieval Christian belief in the face of modern skepticism.

Melville's use of legend differs significantly from Chaucer's use of legend in *The Canterbury Tales* and, for that matter, from his own use of legend in *Moby-Dick*. The basic plot of "The Prioress's Tale" echoes the legend of Hugh of Lincoln, and legends of the great white whale provide the basic plot for *Moby-Dick*, but no particular Christian legend gives *Clarel* its plot. Instead, the pilgrimage provides the structure, and the landmarks the pilgrims visit allow opportunities to recall the legends in which those landmarks figure prominently. Seldom do the legends become fully developed narratives. Most often the narrator describes a place and then briefly alludes to traditional stories associated with it. The brief references to Christian legend serve as a reminder of what had been lost between Chaucer's time and the age of empiricism.

Late in the first book, Clarel, Rolfe, and Vine explore the sights near Jerusalem. Together they climb Mount Olivet, "A thing preëminent in seat, / Whose legend still can touch the heart" (1.34.71–72). Mount

Olivet, in other words, has enough traditional associations to retain the power to move those who visit it. Atop Olivet is the chapel of the Ascension, with a mark on the floor that, according to legend, was Christ's last footprint. Describing the chapel and its legendary associations, the narrator recalls the story of Arculf, a pilgrim (or palmer) who had visited the place ten centuries before. Returning from the Holy Land, Arculf is shipwrecked off the coast of Iona, an island in the Scottish Hebrides where the monastery of St. Columba was located. Adamnan, the abbot of St. Columba, welcomes Arculf, who tells the abbot of the wonders he had witnessed on Mt. Olivet. Arculf's story told, Adamnan snatches his hand and clings "to it like a very child / Thrilled by some wondrous story wild" (1.35.100–101). The lines echo Melville's description of the credulous northern whalemen in *Moby-Dick* who "hearken with a childish fireside interest and awe, to the wild, strange tales of Southern whaling" (*MD* 181). As *Moby-Dick* recreates the sailor's world of legend for landlubbers unfamiliar with the whaleman's workaday world and superstitious beliefs, "Arculf and Adamnan" recreates the medieval Christian's world of legend and belief for skeptical modern readers. There is a key difference between the two, however. The premise of *Moby-Dick* is that the sailor's world can be brought alive for those who do not share his beliefs; in *Clarel* Melville's narrator laments the impossibility of recapturing the legends. "Arculf and Adamnan" closes with one of the poem's most eloquent passages:

> The abbot and the palmer rest:
> The legends follow them and die—
> Those legends which, be it confessed,
> Did nearer bring to them the sky—
> Did nearer woo it to their hope
> Of all that seers and saints avow—
> Than Galileo's telescope
> Can bid it unto prosing Science now.
> (1.35.108–15)

While these lines toll the death of legend, more hopeful passages in *Clarel* suggest that people could still appreciate the old legends as long as they abandoned their skepticism and stopped insisting on empirical proof.

Describing how the Terra Santa monks left Jerusalem and crossed the Kedron ravine on an evening journey to Bethany, the narrator recalls the legends about the Assumption of the Virgin Mary and how the apostles secretly carried her body to the tomb:

> Kedron they cross. Much so might move—
> If legend hold, which none may prove,—
> The remnant of the Twelve which bore
> Down thro' this glen in funeral plight
> The Mother of our Lord by night
> To sepulcher.
> (1.14.65–66)

The legend of the Assumption of the Virgin Mary circulated widely in the oral tradition and was celebrated in the Roman Catholic Church. Melville also may have known the legend from reading Montalembert's *Life of Saint Elizabeth, of Hungary,* a book he gave his cousin Kate Gansevoort Lansing in 1875 and later recommended to his brother-in-law, John C. Hoadley.[9] Saint Elizabeth had seen the Virgin Mary in a vision, and Mary had told her the story of her Assumption. Elizabeth asked Mary if she should keep the story a secret; Mary replied that it should not be revealed to unbelievers, yet neither should it be hidden from the devout and faithful.

As *Clarel* shows, the empiricists posed the greatest threat to the devout and faithful. The Elder, a Scottish Presbyterian who travels with field glasses, surveyor's tape, and pruning knife, tries to "disprove / Legend and site by square and line" (2.1.76–77). Though among the original group of pilgrims, the Elder, unwelcomed by the others, turns back shortly after the pilgrimage begins. Melville more fully developed the figure of the empiricist with Margoth, whose determination, positivism, and brute strength make him a much more imposing force than the Elder. Margoth is absolutely convinced that science should and must debunk old legends. Shortly after meeting the pilgrims, he tells them:

> "Sirs, heed me:
> This total tract," and Esau's hand
> He waved; "the plain—the vale—Lot's sea—
> It needs we scientists remand
> Back from old theologic myth

To geologic hammers."
(2.20.45–50)

Ironically, Rolfe later compares Margoth to a legendary magician when he sees him attempting a late-night geological experiment by the light of his chemical lamp.

"Look how his ray,"
Said Rolfe, "too small for stars to heed,
Strange lights him, reason's sorcerer,
Poor Simon Magus run to seed.
And, yes, 'twas here—or else I err—
The legends claim, that into sea
The old magician flung his book
When life and lore he both forsook:
The evil spell yet lurks, may be."
(2.37.73–81)

Rolfe's juxtaposition of the brilliant lights of the firmament and the scientist's dim lamp aptly conveys the relationship between God's creation and man's attempt to understand it. Rolfe's characterization of Margoth as a kind of degenerate Simon Magus suggests that his activities will doom him to destruction. In legend, Simon Magus always loses to Peter. According to one legend, Simon threw his magic books into the Dead Sea so Peter would not be able to convict him of sorcery. Incensed with Peter's continual victories, Simon eventually boasts that he will ascend to heaven. He launches himself from a great tower, and gravity quickly takes its toll.[10] During the Renaissance, the fall of Simon Magus became an important part of the iconographic tradition. Melville himself saw Pompeo Batoni's *Fall of Simon Magus* in Rome (*J* 112). Rolfe's analogy between Margoth and Simon Magus thus parallels science with black magic. Furthermore, it suggests that legends of the past provide a way of understanding the present. As he continues the analogy, however, Rolfe becomes unsure of himself. He hesitates, admits he may be wrong, expresses hope that Simon's evil spell may still affect Margoth, yet immediately conveys uncertainty.

Among Clarel's fellow pilgrims, only Nehemiah, the aged American millennialist, achieves a level of faith that allows him to believe the Christian legends wholeheartedly:

> Now Nehemiah with wistful heart
> Much heed had given to myths which bore
> Upon that Pentateuchal shore;
> Him could the wilder legend thrill
> With credulous impulse, whose appeal,
> Oblique, touched on his Christian vein.
> (2.38.1–6)

These lines begin "The Sleep-Walker," a canto that tells how Nehemiah arises in his sleep and walks into the Dead Sea, never to be heard from again. While *Clarel*'s attack on empiricism may seem to value blind faith, Nehemiah's fate suggests otherwise. As a kind of sleep-walking, blind faith is ultimately self-destructive. Skepticism can destroy Christian legend, but unquestioning belief in such legends ultimately can destroy the self.

Legends need not rely solely on belief, however. In "The Site of the Passion," Clarel and Vine visit the Garden of Gethsemane. Attempting to speak to Vine, Clarel is dumbstruck: "Tradition, legend, lent such spell / And rapt him in remoteness so" (1.30.31–32). Clarel's religious beliefs do not render him speechless for long. What strikes Clarel are the traditions associated with Gethsemane. The legends of Christ's Passion have been repeated so often over so many centuries that, believe them or not, they have become an important part of the Western tradition. The narrator emphasizes the idea of tradition elsewhere. Describing the legendary stones atop Mount Olivet overlooking Jerusalem where Christ sat and predicted the city's demise, he mentions the "fond traditions" associated with the place (1.33.6). "Traditions," he says another time, are things "beautiful and old / Which with maternal arms enfold / Millions, else orphaned and made poor" (2.1.85–87). Tradition enhances a culture, providing shared stories that enrich the lives of those who tell them across the generations. The idea of tradition provides a way to justify, accept, appreciate, and perpetuate legends independently from belief.

Derwent, the Anglican priest who, with Clarel, Rolfe, and Vine, completes the pilgrimage, accepts his religion without the kind of deep soul-searching Clarel undergoes. Viewing the legendary birthplace of Jesus Christ in Bethlehem, Derwent exclaims, "I trust tradition!" (4.13.200). Though other passages emphasize the importance of tradition, Derwent's words seem insufficient. A priest must do more than merely trust tradition: he must believe in God with all his heart and soul. Yet his belief must be an informed one, one that is the product of much consideration. Derwent's easy acceptance of his religion does not offer Clarel a solution. As the poem ends, Clarel has yet to reconcile his religious doubts.

While simply trusting tradition may seem insufficient in a man of God, appreciating tradition may have been enough for the poet. Herman Melville, unlike his protagonist, seems to have achieved some degree of personal equilibrium toward Christianity by the poem's end. When the year after *Clarel* was published John C. Hoadley sent him a poem he had written that was based on a Christian legend from the time of Marco Polo, Melville responded with great enthusiasm: "Your legend from Marco Polo I had never previously met with. How full of significance it is! And beauty too. These legends of the Old Faith are really wonderful both from their multiplicity and their poetry. They far surpass the stories in the Greek mythologies. Dont you think so? See, for example, the life of St. Elizabeth of Hungary" (*Co* 452). These comments reflect a remarkable shift since the time Melville looked to Homeric times for complacency two decades before. Writing *Clarel* allowed him to understand Christian legend in a way similar to how he understood other legends and myths. He recognized that he did not need to accept the beliefs they exemplified in order to appreciate their aesthetic qualities, their beauty and poetry.

Conclusion

From the publication of *Clarel* until his death a decade and a half later, Herman Melville frequently returned to the past for literary inspiration. Sometimes he recalled his personal past, while at other times he thought about events that had taken place before his birth. These musings greatly influenced his later work, and traces can be seen in *Billy Budd, John Marr and Other Sailors, with Some Sea-Pieces,* and the Burgundy Club sketches. Despite these recollections of the past, Melville did not return to legends as source material for his late writings; he was more interested in stories with a traceable heritage. An example: when Melville visited England in 1849, he talked with an old pensioner at Greenwich who described serving in the Royal Navy during the previous century. Composing *Billy Budd,* Melville, writing about how convicts were let into the navy, cited as his source "an old pensioner in a cocked hat with whom I had a most interesting talk on the terrace at Greenwich, a Baltimore Negro, a Trafalgar man" (*BB* 66). Earlier, Melville had found the Umi legend attractive because it allowed him to link his personal past with Greek myth. His visit to the Holy Land had given him personal contact with the settings of Christian legend that made *Clarel* possible. Late in life, the personal links became more important than the legends. Historical events acquired significance for Melville only if he could somehow link himself to them. Memories of his own experiences took him back to the first third of the nineteenth century; memories of hearing others relate their personal narratives took him back to the eighteenth.[1]

John Marr and Other Sailors, like *Billy Budd,* reflects Melville's habit late in life of indulging in memories, recalling his experiences as a young sailor and wondering what had happened to his former shipmates. Were they still alive? Any of them? Many? The isolated and landlocked John Marr has feelings similar to Melville's own. In the headnote to his title poem, Melville wrote, "Though John Marr's shipmates could not all have departed life, yet as subjects of meditation they were like phantoms of the dead" (*CP* 164). In the volume's later poems, Melville returned to the traditional lore he had known since his sailor days.

The speaker of "Bridegroom Dick," hardly discernible from Melville's own voice, also ponders the fate of his forecastle friends from long ago. The poet poignantly recollects the flogging of a sailor aboard a man-of-war, an episode which had a real-life equivalent in Melville's experience aboard the *United States*. The poet categorizes the sailor as "the Finn who made the great huff" (*CP* 176). This double entendre conveys the sailor's brash challenge to the officers' authority, yet its wording recalls the superstitious idea of Finnish sailors who could control the wind. Seen in light of Melville's personal experience, the line is actually a triple entendre, for it echoes and obliquely commemorates the name of the real-life sailor whom Melville saw flogged, William Hoff. The entendre also creates irony, for the Finns' supernatural control of the wind generally allowed them to control their own destiny. In the superstitious sailor's personal legend that Richard Henry Dana recounted in *Two Years Before the Mast*, for example, the Finn is imprisoned, but he so successfully controls the wind from the brig that the captain succumbs to his demands. In "Bridegroom Dick," the Finn makes a great huff, but he is powerless in the face of the U.S. Navy. Gone are the days when supernatural force could avenge human cruelty.

Later in "Bridegroom Dick," the poet recalls the great ships of the past.

> Hither and thither, blown wide asunder,
> Where's this fleet, I wonder and wonder.
> Slipt their cables, rattled their adieu,
> (Whereaway pointing? to what rendezvous?)
> Out of sight, out of mind, like the crack *Constitution*,
> And many a keel time never shall renew—
> *Bon Homme Dick* o' the buff Revolution,
> The *Black Cockade* and the staunch *True-Blue*.
> (*CP* 180)

Besides their significance to U.S. naval history, some of the ships are also important to Melville's earlier writings. The *Constitution* still held power in Melville's imagination, and its reference here recalls earlier references in his published and private writings. John Paul Jones's *Bon Homme Richard* figured prominently in *Israel Potter*. These lines, therefore, conflate personal history and national history. Here Melville also uses the proverbial phrase "to slip a cable," which meant, figuratively speaking, to die. He had used the phrase in his earlier writing. In *Moby-Dick* Ishmael had discussed the whaling firm Samuel Enderby and Son, declaring, "All honor to the Enderbies, therefore, whose house, I think, exists to the present day; though doubtless the original Samuel must long ago have slipped his cable for the great South Sea of the other world" (*MD* 444). Melville's use of the proverbial phrase in "Bridegroom Dick" follows his characteristically ironic use of proverbs, for slipping a cable was an actual nautical evolution. The infinitive phrase is only proverbial when applied to human beings. Using it here in its proverbial sense and yet applying it to a ship, Melville created irony by way of personification.

John Marr also contains some of Melville's finest short verse. Many use traditional motifs and echo Melville's earlier works. "Far Off-Shore," which describes an empty raft with sea birds hovering over it, recalls the image of the empty life buoy in *White-Jacket,* with its accompanying white sea bird. "The Figure-Head," which W. Clark Russell called "the gem of the collection" (*Co* 744), depicts the *Charles-and-Emma*'s double figurehead, a young married couple. After lengthy service, the couple begins to show the wear of the salt sea:

> But came in end a dismal night,
> With creaking beams and ribs that groan,
> A black lee-shore and waters white:
> Dropped on the reef, the pair lie prone:
> O, the breakers dance, but the winds they moan!
> (*CP* 198)

The poem reflects the idea of a ship's figurehead as its talisman. Furthermore, the wedded couple paradoxically is brought to life in death. Moaning at sea, as the Old Manxman had recognized in *Moby-Dick,* was the sound of souls newly drowned.

No poem in *John Marr* more fully incorporates traditional materials than "Tom Deadlight." A headnote to the poem explains that its speaker is a grizzled petty officer who lies in a sick-bay hammock aboard a British man-of-war returning home from the Mediterranean. Two messmates, Matt and Jock, watch over him. Though Tom's mind wanders, he has glimpses of sanity and "sings by snatches his good-bye and last injunctions" derived "from a famous old sea-ditty." The ditty is "Spanish Ladies," a song Jack Chase had sung aboard the *Neversink,* and a song the *Pequod*'s crew had sung in "Midnight, Forecastle."

The first two stanzas which Tom Deadlight sings closely follow the traditional song, but as his vision blurs and his mind wanders in the third, he thinks he nears the Cape of Good Hope and imagines seeing the legendary Flying Dutchman. As a messmate fans him with a sou'wester, Tom mistakes it for something else:

> But what's this I feel that is fanning my cheek, Matt?
> The white goney's wing?—how she rolls!—'tis the Cape!
> (*CP* 183)

The white goney, or albatross, represents, as it does so often in Melville's writings, the soul of a sailor who dies at sea. Here, Tom feels death so near that his soul seems already to have left his body and is getting ready for its final departure skyward. Tom becomes lucid again as he finishes his song, says good-bye, shakes hands, and suggests customs to be observed in his burial.

> But give me my *tot*, Matt, before I roll over;
> Jock, let's have your flipper, it's good for to feel;
> And don't sew me up without *baccy* in mouth, boys,
> And don't blubber like lubbers when I turn up my keel.
> (*CP* 184)

"Tom Deadlight" combines several traditional genres—burial custom, folksong, legend, superstition—with Melville's personal vision. The poem tells the story of a man who has served aboard a man-of-war and, now approaching death, sees the visions of a lifetime, both real and legendary, flit before him. As Herman Melville late in his life assembled the poems that form *John Marr and Other Sailors,* he too had visions pass before his mind's eye: faces of friends long gone, characters of his own creation, and images from tall tales, legends, and many as real a story.

Notes

1. Superstition and the Sea

1. George Bayley, Letter to Editor, *Gentleman's Magazine* 93 (1823): 16–17.

2. Thomas Q. Couch, "The Folk Lore of a Cornish Village: Witchcraft, Etc.," *Notes and Queries* ser. 1, 11 (30 June 1855): 498. See also Robert Means Lawrence, *The Magic of the Horseshoe with Other Folk-Lore Notes* (1898; reprint, Detroit: Singing Tree Press, 1968), 109–10; and Newbell Niles Puckett, *Popular Beliefs and Superstitions: A Compendium of American Folklore from the Ohio Collection of Newbell Niles Puckett,* ed. Wayland D. Hand, Anna Casetta, and Sondra B. Thiederman (Boston: G. K. Hall, 1981), no. 19084.

3. Vincent Stuckey Lean, *Lean's Collectanea* (Bristol: J. W. Arrowsmith, 1902–4), 2:446.

4. "Sailor's Dread of Friday," *Rose of the Valley* [Cincinnati] 1 (1839): 249, reprinted from the *New York Whig*. See also Fletcher S. Bassett, *Sea Phantoms: or Legends and Superstitions of the Sea and of Sailors in All Lands and at All Times* (Chicago: Morrill, Higgins, 1892), 443–46; Helen Creighton, *Bluenose Magic: Popular Beliefs and Superstitions in Nova Scotia* (Toronto: The Ryerson Press, 1968), 128–29; Francis Allyn Olmstead, *Incidents of a Whaling Voyage to Which Are Added Observations on the Scenery, Manners and Customs, and Missionary Stations of the Sandwich and Society Islands,* ed. W. Storrs Lee (Rutland, VT: Charles E. Tuttle, 1969), 15–16.

5. Margaret Baker, *Folklore of the Sea* (North Pomfret, VT: David & Charles, 1979), 20.

6. The Massachusetts Historical Society in Boston has an excellent collection of canes made from the *Constitution*'s timbers.

7. Baker, *Folklore of the Sea,* 77; Frank C. Brown, *The Frank C. Brown Collection of North Carolina Folklore,* ed. Newman Ivey White (Durham: Duke University Press, 1952–64), nos. 244–45 and sources cited therein; Creighton, *Bluenose Magic,* 144–45.

8. Brown, *North Carolina Folklore,* no. 5631.

9. Herman Melville, "Daniel Orme," *Billy Budd and Other Prose Pieces,* ed. Raymond W. Weaver (1924; reprint, New York: Russell & Russell, 1963), 120.

10. Baker, *Folklore of the Sea,* 81.

11. Puckett, *Popular Beliefs and Superstitions,* no. 19065.

12. Creighton, *Bluenose Magic,* 119.

13. Ibid., 117–19; Arthur Huff Fauset, *Folklore from Nova Scotia* (New York: American Folk-Lore Society, 1931), 180.

14. Creighton, *Bluenose Magic,* 121.

15. Ibid.

16. Ibid., 126.

17. Baker, *Folklore of the Sea*, 24.

18. Brown, *North Carolina Folklore,* nos. 3238–39.

19. Horace Beck, *Folklore and the Sea* (Middletown, CT: Wesleyan University Press, 1973), 300–301; Christina Hole, "Superstitions and Beliefs of the Sea," *Folklore* 78 (1967): 188.

20. Brown, *North Carolina Folklore,* no. 7331; Puckett, *Popular Beliefs and Superstitions,* nos. 19168–71.

21. Beck, *Folklore and the Sea,* 291–92; Hole, "Superstitions," 189; "Popular Superstitions," *New-Yorker* 1 (4 June 1836): 162; Puckett, *Popular Beliefs and Superstitions,* no. 19186; Annie Weston Whitney and Caroline Canfield Bullock, *Folk-Lore from Maryland* (New York: American Folk-Lore Society, 1925), no. 2106. See chapter 7 for further references to Mother Carey's chickens.

22. Geoffrey Sanborn, "The Names of the Devil: Melville's Other Extracts' for *Moby-Dick,*" *Nineteenth-Century Literature* 47 (September 1992): 212–35, convincingly shows that Melville read Francis Palgrave's essay "Superstition and Knowledge" in the *Quarterly Review,* which reviewed of *A Collection of Rare and Curious Tracts on Witchcraft, and the Second Sight.*

23. For an account of the second sight among Manxmen, see A. W. Moore, *The Folk-Lore of the Isle of Man, Being an Account of Its Myths, Legends, Superstitions, Customs, & Proverbs* (1891; reprint, Felinfach: Llanerch Publishers, 1994), 161–63.

24. T. T. Wilkinson, "Scarborough Folk-Lore," *Notes and Queries* ser. 4, 4 (14 August 1869): 131.

25. Baker, *Folklore of the Sea*, 152.

26. T. Rowe, "On Sorcery and Witchcraft," *Gentleman's Magazine* 33 (1763): 14–15.

27. Fanny D. Bergen, *Current Superstitions Collected from the Oral Tradition of English Speaking Folk* (Boston: American Folk-Lore Society/Houghton, Mifflin, 1896), no. 1078; Honoré de Mareville, "Naval Folk Lore," *Notes and Queries* ser. 1, 10 (8 July 1854): 26; Puckett, *Popular Beliefs and Superstitions,* nos. 19119–20; Alex Russell, "Orkney Folk-Lore," *Notes and Queries* ser. 10, 12 (18 December 1909): 483–84; Wilkinson, "Scarborough Folk-Lore," 131.

28. Archer Taylor and Bartlett Jere Whiting, *A Dictionary of American Proverbs and Proverbial Phrases, 1820–1880* (Cambridge, MA: The Belknap Press of Harvard University Press, 1958), 405; Bartlett Jere Whiting, *Modern Proverbs and Proverbial Sayings* (Cambridge, MA: Harvard University Press, 1989), 687.

29. George Oliver, "Popular Superstitions of Lincolnshire," *Gentleman's Magazine* 102 (1832): 592.

30. Kevin J. Hayes, *Folklore and Book Culture* (Knoxville: University of Tennessee Press, 1997), 59–73, *passim.*

31. Mareville, "Naval Folk Lore," 26; Lean, *Lean's Collectanea* 2:185.

32. Richard Henry Dana, *Two Years before the Mast: A Personal Narrative of Life at Sea* (New York: Harper & Brothers, 1840), 49.

2. FICTION AND FOLKSONG

1. Ira W. Ford, *Traditional Music of America* (1940; reprint, New York: Da Capo Press, 1978), 391. Agnes Dicken Cannon, "Melville's Use of Sea Ballads and Songs,"

Western Folklore 23 (1964): 6, briefly discusses Melville's use of "The Bavarian Broomseller."

2. Helen Creighton and Doreen H. Senior, *Traditional Songs from Nova Scotia* (Toronto: Ryerson Press, 1950), 131.

3. Hershel Parker, *Herman Melville: A Biography* (Baltimore: Johns Hopkins University Press, 1996–), 1:636–60, *passim*.

4. William Main Doerflinger, *Shantymen and Shantyboys: Songs of the Sailor and Lumberman* (New York: Macmillan, 1951), 307.

5. Parker, *Herman Melville* 1:269.

6. Francis James Child, *The English and Scottish Popular Ballads* (1882–98; reprint, New York: Dover, 1965), no. 289, variant B. For a good recording of the song, see Paul Clayton, *Whaling and Sailing Songs* (1957; Tradition compact disc, 1997).

7. Child, *English and Scottish Popular Ballads*, no. 58, variant C.

8. For variants see W. Roy Mackenzie, *Ballads and Sea Songs from Nova Scotia* (Cambridge, MA: Harvard University Press, 1928), 257–58 and the references therein.

9. Mackenzie, *Ballads and Sea Songs from Nova Scotia,* 257. In his headnote to the song, Mackenzie provides citations for numerous other recorded variants. For a good recording, see Clayton, *Whaling and Sailing Songs.*

10. Parker, *Herman Melville* 1:271–73.

11. Joanna C. Colcord, *Songs of American Sailormen* (New York: W. W. Norton, 1938), 76. For variants see Frank Shay, *American Sea Songs and Chanteys from the Days of Iron Men and Wooden Ships* (1948; reprint, Plainview, NY: Books for Libraries Press, 1969), 32–33; Laura Alexandrine Smith, *The Music of the Waters: A Collection of the Sailors' Chanties, or Working Songs of the Sea, of All Maritime Nations* (London: Kegan Paul, Trench, 1888), 22–23; and R. H. Whall, *Sea Songs and Shanties* (Glasgow: Brown, Son & Ferguson, 1927), 89–90.

12. Stuart M. Frank, "'Cheerly Man': Chanteying in *Omoo* and *Moby-Dick*," *New England Quarterly* 58 (1985): 72.

3. PROVERB AND IRONY

1. Herman Melville's whereabouts in late September remain uncertain, but Hershel Parker, *Herman Melville: A Biography* (Baltimore: Johns Hopkins University Press, 1996–), 1:180, places him "in New York City, perhaps as early as August 1840, perhaps as late as November." Gansevoort's two surviving *Index Rerum*s are located at the Berkshire Athenaeum, Pittsfield, Massachusetts.

2. Archer Taylor, *The Proverb* (Cambridge, MA: Harvard University Press, 1931), 171–72.

3. Herman Melville, "To Major John Gentian, Dean of the Burgundy Club," in *Billy Budd and Other Prose Pieces,* ed. Raymond W. Weaver (1924; reprint, New York: Russell & Russell, 1963), 358.

4. Ralph Waldo Emerson, *The Collected Works of Ralph Waldo Emerson,* Vol. 4: *Representative Men: Seven Lectures,* ed. Wallace E. Williams and Douglas Emory Wilson (Cambridge, MA: Belknap Press of Harvard University Press, 1987), 90.

5. C. Merton Babcock, "Melville's Proverbs of the Sea," *Western Folklore* 11 (1952): 254.

6. Archer Taylor and Bartlett Jere Whiting, *A Dictionary of American Proverbs*

and Proverbial Phrases, 1820–1880 (Cambridge, MA: The Belknap Press of Harvard University Press, 1958), 126, 403, first identified these two as manufactured proverbs.

7. The best bibliographical overview of *The Way to Wealth* is the headnote to "Poor Richard Improved, 1758," in *The Papers of Benjamin Franklin*, ed. Leonard W. Labaree et al. (New Haven: Yale University Press, 1959–), 7:326–40. There has never been a thorough attempt to catalog all editions. For the most complete listing, see *National Union Catalog: Pre-1956 Imprints* (London: Mansell, 1968–81), nos. F0339527-F0339857.

8. Kevin J. Hayes, *Folklore and Book Culture* (Knoxville: University of Tennessee Press, 1997), 38–41.

9. E. A. Wallis Budge, *Amulets and Talismans* (New Hyde Park, NY: University Books, 1961), 52–53; Hayes, *Folklore and Book Culture*, 35–36.

10. Quoted in *Oxford English Dictionary*, 2d ed.

11. Oliver Goldsmith, *The Vicar of Wakefield*, ed. Ernest Brennecke (New York: Pocket Library, 1957), 3.

12. F. A. Durivage, "The Fastest Funeral on Record," in *A Quarter Race in Kentucky, and Other Sketches, Illustrative of Scenes, Characters, and Incidents, throughout the Universal Yankee Nation*, ed. William T. Porter (Philadelphia: Carey and Hart, 1847), 47–48.

4. Phantom Sailors

1. Leigh Hunt, *The Autobiography of Leigh Hunt*, ed. J. E. Morpurgo (London: Cresset Press, 1949), 295.

2. Richard Henry Dana, *Two Years before the Mast: A Personal Narrative of Life at Sea* (New York: Harper and Brothers, 1840), 50.

3. [Edgar Allan Poe,] review of Frederick Marryat, *The Phantom Ship, Burton's Gentleman's Magazine* 5 (August 1839): 359.

4. Horace Beck, *Folklore and the Sea* (Middletown, CT: Wesleyan University Press, 1973), 283.

5. Ralph Waldo Emerson, "Demonology," in *The Early Lectures of Ralph Waldo Emerson*, ed. Robert E. Spiller and Wallace E. Williams (Cambridge, MA: Belknap Press of Harvard University Press, 1972), 3:157.

6. George Perkins, "Death by Spontaneous Combustion in Marryat, Melville, Dickens, Zola, and Others," *Dickensian* 60 (1964): 57–59, finds a parallel episode in Frederick Marryat's *Jacob Faithful* (1834) but suggests that Melville's source for the idea of spontaneous combustion was John Mason Good's *Book of Nature* (Mary K. Bercaw, *Melville's Sources* [Evanston: Northwestern University Press, 1987], no. 308), a work that White-Jacket calls "a very good book, to be sure, but not precisely adapted to tarry tastes" (*WJ* 167).

7. Kevin J. Hayes, *Folklore and Book Culture* (Knoxville: University of Tennessee Press, 1997), 46.

8. Hershel Parker, *Herman Melville: A Biography* (Baltimore: Johns Hopkins University Press, 1996–), 1:273–74.

9. Margaret Baker, *Folklore of the Sea* (North Pomfret, VT: David & Charles, 1979), 108.

NOTES TO PAGES 47–60

10. Baker, *Folklore of the Sea*, 162; Fletcher S. Bassett, *Sea Phantoms: or Legends and Superstitions of the Sea and of Sailors in All Lands and at All Times* (Chicago: Morrill, Higgins, 1892), 311, 314, 315, 317–18; Vincent Stuckey Lean, *Lean's Collectanea* (Bristol: J. W. Arrowsmith, 1902–4), 2:322.

11. Bassett, *Sea Phantoms*, 305, 310, 312.

5. TALL TALK AND TALL TALES

1. Jay Leyda, *The Melville Log: A Documentary Life of Herman Melville, 1819–1891* (1951; reprint, New York: Gordian Press, 1969), 2:648.

2. Carolyn S. Brown, *The Tall Tale in American Folklore and Literature* (Knoxville: University of Tennessee Press, 1987), 35–36.

3. Bartlett C. Jones, "American Frontier Humor in Melville's *Typee*," *New York Folklore Quarterly* 15 (1959): 283.

4. *Morning Courier and New-York Enquirer* (17 April 1846), as reprinted in Brian Higgins and Hershel Parker, *Herman Melville: The Contemporary Reviews* (New York: Cambridge University Press, 1995), 46.

5. Reviewers for the *Philadelphia Saturday Courier* (4 August 1838) and the *Gentleman's Magazine* (September 1838) compared *Pym* to *Munchausen's Travels.* See Dwight Thomas and David K. Jackson, *The Poe Log: A Documentary Life of Edgar Allan Poe 1809–1849* (Boston: G. K. Hall, 1987), 250, 254.

6. *National Union Catalog: Pre-1956 Imprints* (London: Mansell, 1968–81), M0878617, M0878636–M0878637. Though the 1828 edition is the earliest known edition published by King, an advertisement for Munchausen's *Travels* in King's edition of *Arden, the Unfortunate Stranger* (ca. 1825) may refer to an earlier edition. See Harry B. Weiss, "Solomon King, Early New York Bookseller and Publisher of Children's Books and Chapbooks," *Bulletin of the New York Public Library* 51 (1947): 537.

7. Gérard Genette, *Narrative Discourse: An Essay in Method,* trans. Jane E. Lewin (Ithaca: Cornell University Press, 1980). Neil R. Grobman discusses several occurrences of tall tale as direct discourse in "The Tall Tale Telling Events in Melville's *Moby-Dick*," *Journal of the Folklore Institute* 12 (1975): 19–27.

8. Victor Wolfgang von Hagen, "Introduction," *Incidents of Travel in Egypt, Arabia Petraea, and the Holy Land,* by John Lloyd Stephens (Norman: University of Oklahoma Press, 1970), xxxii; Hershel Parker, "Historical Supplement," in *Clarel: A Poem and Pilgrimage in the Holy Land,* ed. Harrison Hayford, Alma A. MacDougall, Hershel Parker, and G. Thomas Tanselle (Evanston and Chicago: Northwestern University Press and The Newberry Library, 1991), 640–41.

9. James Kirkland, "A New Source for the 'Trepan' Scenes in Melville's *Mardi*," *English Language Notes* 30 (June 1993): 39–40.

10. Neil R. Grobman, "Melville's Use of Tall Tale Humor," *Southern Folklore Quarterly* 40 (1977): 191.

11. For a full discussion of this idea, see Warwick Wadlington, "Ishmael's Godly Gamesomeness: Selftaste and Rhetoric in *Moby-Dick*," in *The Critical Response to Herman Melville's Moby-Dick,* ed. Kevin J. Hayes (Westport, CT: Greenwood Press, 1994), 130–52.

12. *Log* 1:445.

6. REDBURN AND THE CHAPBOOK

1. Kevin J. Hayes, *Folklore and Book Culture* (Knoxville: University of Tennessee Press, 1997), 4–5; Margaret Spufford, *Small Books and Pleasant Histories: Popular Fiction and Its Readership in Seventeenth-Century England* (Athens: University of Georgia Press, 1981), 48–49.

2. OCLC 2891008, 3037118, 34840122.

3. OCLC 15685054, 17356242, 29949124, 30502623.

4. Merton M. Sealts, Jr., *Melville's Reading: Revised and Enlarged Edition* (Columbia: University of South Carolina Press, 1988), no. 232a.

5. OCLC 16693458.

6. Jay Leyda, *The Melville Log: A Documentary Life of Herman Melville, 1819–1891* (1951; reprint, New York: Gordian Press, 1969), 2:507.

7. Samuel King published editions of *Valentin and Orson* in 1825 (OCLC 15147886) and 1828 (OCLC 34599034). See also, A. S. W. Rosenbach, *Early American Children's Books* (1933; reprint, New York: Kraus, 1966), no. 721.

8. Charles Welsh and William H. Tillinghast, *Catalogue of English and American Chapbooks and Broadside Ballads in Harvard College Library* (1905; reprint, Detroit: Singing Tree Press, 1968), 119. Melville also may have known Friar Bacon from Robert Greene's *Friar Bacon and Friar Bungay,* which Robert Dodsley included in his *Select Collection of Old Plays* (Sealts, *Melville's Reading,* no. 188).

9. Clarence Saunders Brigham, "Bibliography of American Editions of Robinson Crusoe to 1830," *Proceedings of the American Antiquarian Society* 67 (1958): 137–83. Wilson L. Heflin, *New Light on Herman Melville's Cruise in the Charles and Henry* (Glassboro, NJ: Melville Society, 1974), 13, shows that there was a children's edition of *Robinson Crusoe* in the ship's library of the *Charles and Henry* when Melville was aboard.

10. John Bryant, *Melville and Repose: The Rhetoric of Humor in the American Renaissance* (New York: Oxford University Press, 1993), 157–60.

11. Gayle Cooper, Scott Bruntjen, and Carol Rinderknecht, *A Checklist of American Imprints for 1830[–1839]* (Metuchen, NJ: Scarecrow Press, 1972–88), no. 2930.

12. Otho T. Beall, Jr. "*Aristotle's Master Piece* in America: A Landmark in the Folklore of Medicine," *William and Mary Quarterly* ser. 3, 20 (1963): 207–22.

13. Keith Huntress, "A Note on Melville's *Redburn,*" *New England Quarterly* 18 (1945): 259, tentatively identifies the work as Andrew Blake's *Delirium Tremens* (London, 1830), but that work was only sixty-eight pages long. Blake's work was abbreviated and reprinted as a twenty-four-page pamphlet in Washington in 1834 (OCLC 6005492). Two other works appeared in the 1830s, Julis Wolff's *Delirium tremens* (London, 1839), a fifty-page pamphlet (OCLC 19792614), and John Ware's *Remarks on the History and Treatment of Delirium Tremens* (Boston, 1831), a sixty-one-page pamphlet (OCLC 13387378).

14. "Political Economy," *Aurora* [Philadelphia] 1 (19 July 1835): 13–14.

15. Hayes, *Folklore and Book Culture,* 32.

16. Ibid., 15.

17. Maxine Moore, *That Lonely Game: Melville, Mardi, and the Almanac* (Columbia: University of Missouri Press, 1975), first identified Jack Blunt's Dream Book as *Napoleon's Book of Fate.* Susan Vanzanten Gallagher, apparently unaware of Moore's work, identified it again in "Jack Blunt and His Dream Book," *American Literature* 58

(1986): 614–19. Neither examined a copy of the work, however. Information in the following discussion is from *The Book of Fate Formerly in the Possession of and Used by Napoleon*, trans. H. Kirchenhoffer (1822; reprint, Scranton, PA: Personal Arts, 1927) and will not be separately documented.

18. Richard Henry Dana, *Two Years before the Mast: A Personal Narrative of Life at Sea* (New York: Harper and Brothers, 1840), 50.

19. Harry B. Weiss, "American Editions of 'Sir Richard Whittington and His Cat,'" *Bulletin of the New York Public Library* 42 (1938): 485.

7. *MOBY-DICK,* LEGEND IN THE MAKING

1. Richard M. Dorson, *American in Legend: Folklore from the Colonial Period to the Present* (New York: Pantheon, 1973), 92–98.

2. In Hershel Parker, *Herman Melville: A Biography* (Baltimore: Johns Hopkins University Press, 1996–), 1:434.

3. [Nathaniel Hawthorne,] "Sketches from Memory," *New-England Magazine* 9 (December 1835): 406–7.

4. Parker, *Herman Melville* 1:696.

5. *Detroit Free Press,* 3 April 1892, as reprinted in John Freeman, *Herman Melville* (New York: Macmillan, 1926), 189–95.

6. William Comstock, *A Voyage to the Pacific, Descriptive of the Customs, Usages, and Sufferings on Board of Nantucket Whale-Ships* (Boston: Oliver L. Perkins, 1838), 45; Ralph Waldo Emerson, *The Journals and Miscellaneous Notebooks of Ralph Waldo Emerson,* ed. Alfred R. Ferguson (Cambridge, MA: Belknap Press of Harvard University Press, 1964), 4:265; J. N. Reynolds, "Mocha Dick; or the White Whale of the Pacific: A Leaf from a Manuscript Journal," *Knickerbocker* 13 (1839): 379.

7. S. Compton Smith, "Spotted Bob: A Forecastle Yarn," in Robert C. Craven, "Two New Sightings of the White Whale," *Melville Society Extracts* no. 63 (September 1985): 13–16; Luther S. Mansfield and Howard P. Vincent, "Explanatory Notes," in *Moby-Dick* (New York: Hendricks House, 1952), 720.

8. Smith, "Spotted Bob," 15.

9. Ibid.

10. Comstock, *Voyage to the Pacific,* 51–52; Emerson, *Journals* 4:265; Reynolds, "Mocha Dick," 379.

11. Deborah C. Andrews, "Attacks of Whales on Ships: A Checklist, *Extracts* no. 18 (1974): 3–17.

12. Emerson, *Journals* 4:265.

13. J. Ross Browne, *Etchings of a Whaling Cruise,* ed. John Seelye (Cambridge, MA: Belknap Press of Harvard University Press, 1968), 448.

14. Mansfield and Vincent, "Explanatory Notes," 721.

15. For the best survey of legend theory, see Timothy R. Tangherlini, "'It Happened Not Too Far From Here . . .': A Survey of Legend Theory and Characterization," *Western Folklore* 49 (October 1990): 371–90.

16. Charles Burchfield, *Charles Burchfield's Journals: The Poetry of Place,* ed. J. Benjamin Townsend (Albany: State University of New York Press, 1993), 660.

17. Helen Creighton, *Bluenose Magic: Popular Beliefs and Superstitions in Nova Scotia* (Toronto: Ryerson Press, 1968), 119; Luis Marden, "Restoring Old Ironsides,"

National Geographic 191 (June 1997): 49.

18. Arthur Huff Fauset, *Folklore from Nova Scotia* (New York: American Folk-Lore Society, 1931), 189.

19. The quotation here incorporates an emendation that I have made to the text of *Moby-Dick*, the first edition of which reads "Surgeon's Astronomy." This mistranscription has been perpetuated in every subsequent edition of *Moby-Dick*, for Melville surely wrote "Ferguson's Astronomy." James Ferguson's *Easy Introduction to Astronomy, for Young Gentlemen and Ladies* had been the most widely read astronomy textbook since the late colonial period (see Kevin J. Hayes, *A Colonial Woman's Bookshelf* [Knoxville: University of Tennessee Press, 1996], 129); Allan Melvill's copy of the work survived in the family (see Merton M. Sealts, Jr., *Melville's Reading: Revised and Enlarged Edition* [Columbia: University of South Carolina Press, 1988], no. 214).

20. Augustus De Morgan, *A Budget of Paradoxes,* ed. David Eugene Smith, 2d ed. (Chicago: Open Court, 1915), 1:42n.

21. Thomas Pynchon, *V* (1961; reprint, New York: Harper and Row, 1986), 39–40.

22. Parker, *Herman Melville* 1:793, locates the reference to "Home Oracles" but does not identify the work.

23. *London Leader,* 8 November 1851, 1067–68, as reprinted in Hershel Parker and Harrison Hayford, eds., *Moby-Dick as Doubloon: Essays and Extracts (1851–1970)* (New York: W. W. Norton, 1970), 26. While the editors of *Doubloon* do not attribute the review to Lewes, Lewes's editor had made the attribution some years before. See Alice R. Kaminsky, *Literary Criticism of George Henry Lewes* (Lincoln: University of Nebraska Press, 1964), 106–7.

24. Laura Alexandrine Smith, *The Music of the Waters: A Collection of the Sailors' Chanties, or Working Songs of the Sea, of All Maritime Nations* (London: Kegan Paul, Trench, 1888), 337.

25. Sidney Oldall Addy, *Household Tales with Other Traditional Remains Collected in the Counties of York, Lincoln, Derby, and Nottingham* (London: David Nutt, 1895), 73.

26. *London Atlas,* 8 November 1851, as reprinted in Parker and Hayford, *Doubloon,* 22.

27. Robert Buchanan, "Melville, Sea-Compelling Man," in Brian Higgins and Hershel Parker, eds., *Critical Essays on Herman Melville's Moby-Dick* (New York: G. K. Hall, 1992), 91.

8. LEGEND, BELIEF, TRADITION, AND *CLAREL*

1. Jay Leyda, *The Melville Log: A Documentary Life of Herman Melville, 1819–1891* (1951; reprint, New York: Gordian Press, 1969), 2:676–77, 804.

2. Ruth Blair, "Melville and Hawaii: Reflections on a New Melville Letter," *Studies in the American Renaissance, 1995,* ed. Joel Myerson (Charlottesville: University Press of Virginia, 1995), 229–50.

3. Journal of John Thomas Gulick, as extracted in *Log* 2:605.

4. Nathaniel Hawthorne, *The English Notebooks, 1856–1860,* ed. Thomas Woodson and Bill Ellis (Columbus: Ohio State University Press, 1997), 163.

5. For the best survey of the composition of *Clarel,* see Hershel Parker, "Historical Supplement," in *Clarel: A Poem and Pilgrimage in the Holy Land,* ed. Harrison

Hayford, Alma A. MacDougall, Hershel Parker, and G. Thomas Tanselle (Evanston and Chicago: Northwestern University Press and The Newberry Library, 1991), 651–55.

6. Merton M. Sealts, Jr., *Melville's Reading: Revised and Enlarged Edition* (Columbia: University of South Carolina Press, 1988), nos. 143, 342.

7. Bernard Rosenthal, "Herman Melville's Wandering Jews," in *Puritan Influences in American Literature,* ed. Emory Elliot (Urbana: University of Illinois Press, 1979), 167–92.

8. Walker Cowen, *Melville's Marginalia* (New York: Garland, 1987), 1:462.

9. Merton M. Sealts, Jr., *Melville's Reading: Revised and Enlarged Edition* (Columbia: University of South Carolina Press, 1988), no. 368.

10. E. M. Butler, *The Myth of the Magus* (New York: Macmillan, 1948), 73–83.

CONCLUSION

1. Hershel Parker, *Reading Billy Budd* (Evanston: Northwestern University Press, 1990), 13–14.

Sources

Aarne, Antti, and Stith Thompson. *The Types of the Folktale: A Classification and Bibliography . . . Second Revision.* Helsinki: Suomalainen Tiedeakatemia Academia Scientarum Fennica, 1961.

Addy, Sidney Oldall. *Household Tales with Other Traditional Remains Collected in the Counties of York, Lincoln, Derby, and Nottingham.* London: David Nutt, 1895.

Andrews, Deborah C. "Attacks of Whales on Ships: A Checklist." *Extracts* no. 18 (1974): 3–17.

Babcock, C. Merton. "Melville's Backwoods Seamen." *Western Folklore* 10 (1951): 126–33.

———. "Melville's Proverbs of the Sea." *Western Folklore* 11 (1952): 254–65.

Baker, Margaret. *Folklore of the Sea.* North Pomfret, VT: David & Charles, 1979.

Bassett, Fletcher S. *Legends and Superstitions of the Sea and of Sailors in All Lands and at All Times.* Chicago: Belford, Clarke, 1885.

———. *Sea Phantoms: or Legends and Superstitions of the Sea and of Sailors in All Lands and at All Times.* Chicago: Morrill, Higgins, 1892.

Bayley, George. Letter to Editor. *Gentleman's Magazine* 93 (1823): 16–17.

Beall, Otho T., Jr. "*Aristotle's Master Piece* in America: A Landmark in the Folklore of Medicine." *William and Mary Quarterly* ser. 3, 20 (1963): 207–22.

Beck, Horace. *Folklore and the Sea.* Middletown, CT: Wesleyan University Press, 1973.

Bercaw, Mary K. *Melville's Sources.* Evanston: Northwestern University Press, 1987.

Bergen, Fanny D. *Current Superstitions Collected from the Oral Tradition of English Speaking Folk.* Boston: American Folk-Lore Society/Houghton, Mifflin, 1896.

SOURCES

Bergmann, Johannes Dietrich. "The Original Confidence Man." *American Quarterly* 21 (Fall 1969): 560–77.

Blair, Ruth. "Melville and Hawaii: Reflections on a New Melville Letter." *Studies in the American Renaissance, 1995.* Ed. Joel Myerson. Charlottesville: University Press of Virginia, 1995. 229–50.

The Book of Fate Formerly in the Possession of and Used by Napoleon. Trans. H. Kirchenhoffer. 1822. Reprint. Scranton, PA: Personal Arts, 1927.

Brigham, Clarence Saunders. "Bibliography of American Editions of Robinson Crusoe to 1830." *Proceedings of the American Antiquarian Society* 67 (1958): 137–83.

Brown, Carolyn S. *The Tall Tale in American Folklore and Literature.* Knoxville: University of Tennessee Press, 1987.

Brown, Frank C. *The Frank C. Brown Collection of North Carolina Folklore.* Ed. Newman Ivey White et al. 7 vols. Durham: Duke University Press, 1952–64.

Browne, J. Ross. *Etchings of a Whaling Cruise.* Ed. John Seelye. Cambridge: Belknap Press of Harvard University Press, 1968.

Browne, Ray. Review of Hershel Parker, *Herman Melville: A Biography. Journal of American Culture* 19 (Winter 1996): 124–25.

Bryant, John. *Melville and Repose: The Rhetoric of Humor in the American Renaissance.* New York: Oxford University Press, 1993.

Budge, E. A. Wallis. *Amulets and Talismans.* New Hyde Park, NY: University Books, 1961.

Burchfield, Charles. *Charles Burchfield's Journals: The Poetry of Place.* Ed. J. Benjamin Townsend. Albany: State University of New York Press, 1993.

Butler, E. M. *The Myth of the Magus.* New York: Macmillan, 1948.

Cannon, Agnes Dicken. "Melville's Use of Sea Ballads and Songs." *Western Folklore* 23 (1964): 1–16.

Carpenter, Charles. *History of American Schoolbooks.* Philadelphia: University of Pennsylvania Press, 1963.

Chase, Richard. *Herman Melville: A Critical Study.* New York: Macmillan, 1949.

Child, Francis James. *The English and Scottish Popular Ballads.* 5 vols. 1882–98. Reprint. New York: Dover, 1965.

Clayton, Paul. *Whaling and Sailing Songs from the Days of Moby Dick.* Tradition phonograph album, 1957. Reissued as *Whaling and Sailing Songs.* Tradition compact disc, 1997.

SOURCES

Colcord, Joanna C. *Songs of American Sailormen*. New York: W.W. Norton, 1938.

Comstock, William. *A Voyage to the Pacific, Descriptive of the Customs, Usages, and Sufferings on Board of Nantucket Whale-Ships*. Boston: Oliver L. Perkins, 1838. Reprinted in Joel Myerson. "Comstock's White Whale and *Moby-Dick*." *American Transcendental Quarterly* 29 (1976): 8–27.

Cooper, Gayle, Scott Bruntjen, and Carol Rinderknecht. *A Checklist of American Imprints for 1830[–1839]*. Metuchen, New Jersey: Scarecrow Press, 1972–88.

Couch, Thomas Q. "The Folk Lore of a Cornish Village: Witchcraft, Etc." *Notes and Queries* ser. 1, 11 (30 June 1855): 497–99.

Cowen, Walker. *Melville's Marginalia*. 2 vols. New York: Garland, 1987.

Craven, Robert C. "Two New Sightings of the White Whale." *Melville Society Extracts* no. 63 (September 1985): 12–16.

Creighton, Helen. *Bluenose Magic: Popular Beliefs and Superstitions in Nova Scotia*. Toronto: Ryerson Press, 1968.

Creighton, Helen, and Doreen H. Senior. *Traditional Songs from Nova Scotia*. Toronto: Ryerson Press, 1950.

Dana, Richard Henry. *Two Years before the Mast: A Personal Narrative of Life at Sea*. New York: Harper and Brothers, 1840.

De Morgan, Augustus. *A Budget of Paradoxes*. 2d ed. Ed. David Eugene Smith. 2 vols. Chicago: Open Court, 1915.

Doerflinger, William Main. *Shantymen and Shantyboys: Songs of the Sailor and Lumberman*. New York: Macmillan, 1951.

Dorson, Richard M. *American in Legend: Folklore from the Colonial Period to the Present*. New York: Pantheon, 1973.

———. *Buying the Wind*. Chicago: University of Chicago Press, 1964.

Durivage, F. A. "The Fastest Funeral on Record." In *A Quarter Race in Kentucky, and Other Sketches, Illustrative of Scenes, Characters, and Incidents, throughout the Universal Yankee Nation*. Ed. William T. Porter. Philadelphia: Carey and Hart, 1847. 47–51.

Emerson, Ralph Waldo. *The Collected Works of Ralph Waldo Emerson*. Vol. 4: *Representative Men: Seven Lectures*. Ed. Wallace E. Williams and Douglas Emory Wilson. Cambridge, MA: Belknap Press of Harvard University Press, 1987.

———. "Demonology." In *The Early Lectures of Ralph Waldo Emerson*. Ed. Robert E. Spiller and Wallace E. Williams. Cambridge, MA: Belknap Press of Harvard University Press, 1972. 3:151–71.

SOURCES

————. *The Journals and Miscellaneous Notebooks of Ralph Waldo Emerson.* Vol. 4. Ed. Alfred R. Ferguson. Cambridge, MA: Belknap Press of Harvard University Press, 1964.

Fauset, Arthur Huff. *Folklore from Nova Scotia.* New York: American Folk-Lore Society, 1931.

Ford, Ira W. *Traditional Music of America.* 1940. Reprint. New York: Da Capo Press, 1978.

Frank, Stuart M. "'Cheerly Man': Chanteying in *Omoo* and *Moby-Dick.*" *New England Quarterly* 58 (1985): 68–82.

Freeman, John. *Herman Melville.* New York: Macmillan, 1926.

Gallagher, Susan Vanzanten. "Jack Blunt and His Dream Book." *American Literature* 58 (1986): 614–19.

Genette, Gérard. *Narrative Discourse: An Essay in Method.* Trans. Jane E. Lewin. Ithaca: Cornell University Press, 1980.

Goldsmith, Oliver. *The Vicar of Wakefield.* Ed. Ernest Brennecke. New York: Pocket Library, 1957.

Grobman, Neil R. "Melville's Use of Tall Tale Humor." *Southern Folklore Quarterly* 40 (1977): 183–94.

————. "The Tall Tale Telling Events in Melville's *Moby-Dick.*" *Journal of the Folklore Institute* 12 (1975): 19–27.

Hawthorne, Nathaniel. *The American Notebooks.* Ed. Claude M. Simpson. Columbus: Ohio State University Press, 1972.

————. *The English Notebooks, 1856–1860.* Ed. Thomas Woodson and Bill Ellis. Columbus: Ohio State University Press, 1997.

[————.] "Sketches from Memory." *New-England Magazine* 9 (December 1835): 398–409.

Hayes, Kevin. *A Colonial Woman's Bookshelf.* Knoxville: University of Tennessee Press, 1996.

————, ed. *The Critical Response to Herman Melville's Moby-Dick.* Westport, CT: Greenwood Press, 1994.

————. *Folklore and Book Culture.* Knoxville: University of Tennessee Press, 1997.

Heflin, Wilson L. *New Light on Herman Melville's Cruise in the Charles and Henry.* Glassboro, NJ: Melville Society, 1974.

Higgins, Brian, and Hershel Parker, eds. *Critical Essays on Herman Melville's Moby-Dick.* New York: G. K. Hall, 1992.

————, eds. *Herman Melville: The Contemporary Reviews.* New York: Cambridge University Press, 1995.

Hoffman, Daniel. *Form and Fable in American Fiction.* 1961. Reprint. New York: W. W. Norton, 1973.

Hole, Christina. "Superstitions and Beliefs of the Sea." *Folklore* 78 (1967): 184–89.

Hunt, Leigh. *The Autobiography of Leigh Hunt.* Ed. J. E. Morpurgo. London: Cresset Press, 1949.

Huntress, Keith. "A Note on Melville's *Redburn.*" *New England Quarterly* 18 (1945): 259–60.

Jones, Bartlett C. "American Frontier Humor in Melville's *Typee.*" *New York Folklore Quarterly* 15 (1959): 283–88.

Jones, Steven Swann. *Folklore and Literature in the United States: An Annotated Bibliography of Studies of Folklore in American Literature.* New York: Garland, 1984.

Kirkland, James. "A New Source for the 'Trepan' Scenes in Melville's *Mardi.*" *English Language Notes* 30 (June 1993): 39–47.

Lawrence, Robert Means. *The Magic of the Horseshoe with Other Folk-Lore Notes.* 1898. Reprint. Detroit: Singing Tree Press, 1968.

Lean, Vincent Stuckey. *Lean's Collectanea.* 4 vols. Bristol: J. W. Arrowsmith, 1902–4.

Leyda, Jay. *The Melville Log: A Documentary Life of Herman Melville, 1819–1891.* 1951. Reprint. New York: Gordian Press, 1969. Abbreviated as *Log.*

Mackenzie, W. Roy. *Ballads and Sea Songs from Nova Scotia.* Cambridge, MA: Harvard University Press, 1928.

Mansfield, Luther S., and Howard P. Vincent. "Explanatory Notes." In *Moby-Dick.* By Herman Melville. New York: Hendricks House, 1952.

———. *Moby-Dick: Or, The Whale.* Ed. Luther S. Mansfield and Howard P. Vincent. New York: Hendricks House, 1952.

Marden, Luis. "Restoring Old Ironsides." *National Geographic* 191 (June 1997): 38–53.

Mareville, Honoré de. "Naval Folk Lore." *Notes and Queries* ser. 1, 10 (8 July 1854): 26.

Melville, Herman. *Billy Budd and Other Prose Pieces.* Ed. Raymond W. Weaver. 1924. Reprint. New York: Russell & Russell, 1963.

———. *Billy Budd, Sailor (An Inside Narrative).* Ed. Harrison Hayford and Merton M. Sealts, Jr. Chicago: University of Chicago Press, 1962.

———. *Clarel: A Poem and Pilgrimage in the Holy Land.* Ed. Harrison Hayford, Alma A. MacDougall, Hershel Parker, and G. Thomas

Tanselle. Evanston and Chicago: Northwestern University Press and The Newberry Library, 1991.

———. *Collected Poems of Herman Melville*. Ed. Howard P. Vincent. Chicago: Hendricks House, 1947.

———. *The Confidence-Man: His Masquerade*. Ed. Harrison Hayford, Hershel Parker, and G. Thomas Tanselle. Evanston and Chicago: Northwestern University Press and The Newberry Library, 1984.

———. *Correspondence*. Ed. Lynn Horth. Evanston and Chicago: Northwestern University Press and The Newberry Library, 1993.

———. *Israel Potter: His Fifty Years of Exile*. Ed. Harrison Hayford, Hershel Parker, and G. Thomas Tanselle. Evanston and Chicago: Northwestern University Press and The Newberry Library, 1982.

———. *Journals*. Ed. Howard C. Horsford and Lynn Horth. Evanston and Chicago: Northwestern University Press and The Newberry Library, 1989.

———. *Mardi and a Voyage Thither*. Ed. Harrison Hayford, Hershel Parker, and G. Thomas Tanselle. Evanston and Chicago: Northwestern University Press and The Newberry Library, 1970.

———. *Moby-Dick: Or, The Whale*. Ed. Harrison Hayford, Hershel Parker, and G. Thomas Tanselle. Evanston and Chicago: Northwestern University Press and The Newberry Library, 1988.

———. *Omoo: A Narrative of Adventures in the South Seas*. Ed. Harrison Hayford, Hershel Parker, and G. Thomas Tanselle. Evanston and Chicago: Northwestern University Press and The Newberry Library, 1968.

———. *The Piazza Tales and Other Prose Pieces, 1839–1860*. Ed. Harrison Hayford, Alma A. MacDougall, and G. Thomas Tanselle. Evanston and Chicago: Northwestern University Press and The Newberry Library, 1987.

———. *Redburn: His First Voyage, Being the Sailor-Boy Confessions and Reminiscences of the Son-of-a-Gentleman, in the Merchant Service*. Ed. Harrison Hayford, Hershel Parker, and G. Thomas Tanselle. Evanston and Chicago: Northwestern University Press and The Newberry Library, 1969.

———. *Typee: A Peep at Polynesian Life*. Ed. Harrison Hayford, Hershel Parker, and G. Thomas Tanselle. Evanston and Chicago: Northwestern University Press and The Newberry Library, 1968.

———. *White-Jacket: Or, The World in a Man-of-War*. Ed. Harrison

Hayford, Hershel Parker, and G. Thomas Tanselle. Evanston and Chicago: Northwestern University Press and The Newberry Library, 1970.

Moore, A. W. *The Folk-Lore of the Isle of Man, Being an Account of Its Myths, Legends, Superstitions, Customs, & Proverbs*. 1891. Reprint. Felinfach: Llanerch Publishers, 1994.

Moore, Maxine. *That Lonely Game: Melville, Mardi, and the Almanac*. Columbia: University of Missouri Press, 1975.

Mushabac, Jane. *Melville's Humor: A Critical Study*. Hamden, CT: Archon, 1981.

National Union Catalog: Pre-1956 Imprints. 754 vols. London: Mansell, 1968–81.

Oliver, George. "Popular Superstitions of Lincolnshire." *Gentleman's Magazine* 102 (1832): 590–93.

Olmstead, Francis Allyn. *Incidents of a Whaling Voyage to Which Are Added Observations on the Scenery, Manners and Customs, and Missionary Stations of the Sandwich and Society Islands*. Ed. W. Storrs Lee. Rutland, VT: Charles E. Tuttle, 1969.

Opie, Iona, and Moira Tatem, eds. *A Dictionary of Superstitions*. New York: Oxford University Press, 1989.

[Palgrave, Francis.] "Superstition and Knowledge." Review of *A Collection of Rare and Curious Tracts on Witchcraft, and the Second Sight* and *The Famous Historie of Friar Bacon*. *Quarterly Review* 29 (July 1823): 440–75.

Parker, Hershel. *Herman Melville: A Biography*. Baltimore: Johns Hopkins University Press, 1996–.

———. "Herman Melville's *The Isle of the Cross:* A Survey and a Chronology." *American Literature* 62 (1990): 1–16.

———. "Historical Supplement." In *Clarel: A Poem and Pilgrimage in the Holy Land*. Ed. Harrison Hayford, Alma A. MacDougall, Hershel Parker, and G. Thomas Tanselle. Evanston and Chicago: Northwestern University Press and The Newberry Library, 1991. 639–73.

———. *Reading Billy Budd*. Evanston: Northwestern University Press, 1990.

Parker, Hershel, and Harrison Hayford, eds. *Moby-Dick as Doubloon: Essays and Extracts (1851–1970)*. New York: W. W. Norton, 1970.

Perkins, George. "Death by Spontaneous Combustion in Marryat, Melville, Dickens, Zola, and Others." *Dickensian* 60 (1964): 57–63.

Poe, Edgar Allan. Review of Frederick Marryat, *The Phantom Ship*. *Burton's Gentleman's Magazine* 5 (August 1839): 358–59.

"Political Economy." *Aurora* [Philadelphia] 1 (19 July 1835): 13–14.

"Popular Superstitions." *New-Yorker* 1 (4 June 1836): 162.

Puckett, Newbell Niles. *Popular Beliefs and Superstitions: A Compendium of American Folklore from the Ohio Collection of Newbell Niles Puckett*. Ed. Wayland D. Hand, Anna Casetta, and Sondra B. Thiederman. 3 vols. Boston: G. K. Hall, 1981.

Pynchon, Thomas. *V.* 1961. Reprint. New York: Harper and Row, 1986.

Reynolds, J. N. "Mocha Dick; or the White Whale of the Pacific: A Leaf from a Manuscript Journal." *Knickerbocker* 13(1839): 377–92.

Rosenbach, A. S. W. *Early American Children's Books*. 1933. Reprint. New York: Kraus, 1966.

Rosenthal, Bernard. "Herman Melville's Wandering Jews." In *Puritan Influences in American Literature*. Ed. Emory Elliot. Urbana: University of Illinois Press, 1979. 167–92.

Rourke, Constance. *American Humor: A Study of the National Character*. New York: Harcourt, Brace, 1931.

Rowe, T. "On Sorcery and Witchcraft." *Gentleman's Magazine* 33 (1763): 12–15.

Russell, Alex. "Orkney Folk-Lore." *Notes and Queries* ser. 10, 12 (18 December 1909): 483–84.

"Sailor's Dread of Friday." *Rose of the Valley* [Cincinnati] 1 (1839): 249.

Sanborn, Geoffrey. "The Names of the Devil: Melville Other 'Extracts' for *Moby-Dick*." *Nineteenth-Century Literature* 47 (1992): 212–35.

Schwendinger, Robert J. "The Language of the Sea: Relationships between the Language of Herman Melville and Sea Shanties of the 19th Century." *Southern Folklore Quarterly* 37 (1973): 53–73.

Sealts, Merton M., Jr. *Melville's Reading: Revised and Enlarged Edition*. Columbia: University of South Carolina Press, 1988.

Seelye, John. *Melville: The Ironic Diagram*. Evanston: Northwestern University Press, 1970.

Shakespeare, William. *The Riverside Shakespeare*. Ed. G.Blakemore Evans. Boston: Houghton Mifflin, 1974.

Shaw, Ralph R., and Richard H. Shoemaker. *American Bibliography: A Preliminary Checklist for 1801[–1819]*. New York: Scarecrow Press, 1958–63.

Shay, Frank. *American Sea Songs and Chanteys from the Days of Iron*

Men and Wooden Ships. 1948. Reprint. Plainview, NY: Books for Libraries Press, 1969.

Shoemaker, Richard H. *A Checklist of American Imprints for 1820[–1829]*. New York: Scarecrow Press, 1964–71.

Smith, Laura Alexandrine. *The Music of the Waters: A Collection of the Sailors' Chanties, or Working Songs of the Sea, of All Maritime Nations*. London: Kegan Paul, Trench, 1888.

Smith, S. Compton. "Spotted Bob: A Forecastle Yarn." In Robert C. Craven. "Two New Sightings of the White Whale." *Melville Society Extracts* no. 63 (September 1985): 13–16.

Spufford, Margaret. *Small Books and Pleasant Histories: Popular Fiction and Its Readership in Seventeenth-Century England*. Athens: University of Georgia Press, 1981.

Stanonik, Janez. *Moby Dick: The Myth and the Symbol, A Study in Folklore and Literature*. Ljubljana, Yugoslavia: Ljubljana University Press, 1962.

Tangherlini, Timothy R. "'It Happened Not Too Far From Here . . .': A Survey of Legend Theory and Characterization." *Western Folklore* 49 (October 1990): 371–90.

Taylor, Archer. *The Proverb*. Cambridge, MA: Harvard University Press, 1931.

Taylor, Archer, and Bartlett Jere Whiting. *A Dictionary of American Proverbs and Proverbial Phrases, 1820–1880*. Cambridge, MA: The Belknap Press of Harvard University Press, 1958.

Thomas, Dwight, and David K. Jackson. *The Poe Log: A Documentary Life of Edgar Allan Poe 1809-1849*. Boston: G. K. Hall, 1987.

Thompson, Stith. *Motif-Index of Folk-Literature: A Classification of Narrative Elements in Folktales, Ballads, Myths, Fables, Mediaeval Romances, Exempla, Fabliaux, Jest-Books, and Local Legends*. Rev. ed. 6 vols. Bloomington: Indiana University Press, 1955–58.

Vincent, Howard P. *The Trying-Out of Moby-Dick*. 1949. Reprint. Kent, OH: Kent State University Press, 1980.

Von Hagen, Victor Wolfgang. "Introduction." *Incidents of Travel in Egypt, Arabia Petraea, and the Holy Land*. By John Lloyd Stephens. Norman: University of Oklahoma Press, 1970.

Wadlington, Warwick. "Ishmael's Godly Gamesomeness: Selftaste and Rhetoric in *Moby-Dick*." In *The Critical Response to Herman Melville's Moby-Dick*. Ed. Kevin J. Hayes. Westport, CT: Greenwood Press, 1994. 130–52.

SOURCES

Weiss, Harry B. "American Chapbooks, 1722–1842." *Bulletin of the New York Public Library* 49 (1945): 491–98, 587–95.

———. "American Editions of 'Sir Richard Whittington and His Cat.'" *Bulletin of the New York Public Library* 42 (1938): 477–85.

———. "Solomon King, Early New York Bookseller and Publisher of Children's Books and Chapbooks." *Bulletin of the New York Public Library* 51 (1947): 531–544.

Whall, R. H. *Sea Songs and Shanties.* Glasgow: Brown, Son & Ferguson, 1927.

Whiting, Bartlett Jere. *Modern Proverbs and Proverbial Sayings.* Cambridge, MA: Harvard University Press, 1989.

Whitney, Annie Weston, and Caroline Canfield Bullock. *Folk-Lore from Maryland.* New York: American Folk-Lore Society, 1925.

Wilkinson, T. T. "Scarborough Folk-Lore." *Notes and Queries* ser. 4, 4 (14 August 1869): 131–32.

Index

INDEX

Browne, J. Ross, *Etchings of a Whaling Cruise,* 78
Browne, Ray, xi
Browne, Thomas, 81–82, 95; *Vulgar Errors,* 95; *Works,* 73
Bryant, John, ix
Buchanan, Robert, 91
Bulwer-Lytton, Edward, *Pilgrims of the Rhine,* 25–26
Burchfield, Charles, 83
Burgundy Club sketches, 27, 103
Burial customs, xi, 39–40, 45–46, 106
Burton, Robert, 81–82; *Anatomy of Melancholy,* 47, 73

Cable, "to slip a cable" (proverbial phrase), 104–5
Calm, "the calm before the storm" (proverb), 37
Camoens, 18; *Lusiad,* 47
Cannon, Agnes Dicken, xi
Cape of Good Hope, 9, 106
Cape Hatteras, 3
Cape Horn, 3, 9, 11, 39, 51, 59
Cape May, 52
Caul, 3
Chapbooks, xii, 32, 52, 62–76, 81
Charms, 1–3, 5, 33, 40, 66, 84, 87. *See also* Amulets; Talismans; specific objects used as such
Chase, Jack, 2, 6, 9, 18–20, 96, 106
Chase, Owen, *Narrative of the . . . Essex,* 80
Chase, Richard, *Herman Melville: A Critical Study,* ix
Chaucer, Geoffrey, 18, 96; *Canterbury Tales,* 97; "The Prioress's Tale," 96
"Cheerly, Man" (shanty), 20–22
Chicks, "don't count your chicks before they are hatched" (proverb), 32
Child, Francis James, *English and Scottish Ballads,* 95–96
Children's books, xii, 63–65
Christian legend, xiii, 92–102
Clarel, x–xi, xiii, 2, 4, 29, 48, 89, 92–103

—Cantos: "Arculf and Adamnan," 98; "The Masque," 96; "The Site of the Passion," 101; "The Sleep–Walker," 100–101
—characters: Agath, 2, 4–5, 48; Belex, 71; Clarel, x, 97–98, 100–102; Derwent, 101–2; Djalea, 71; The Elder, 99; Margoth, 99–100; Nehemiah, 71, 100–101; Rolfe, 89, 97, 100–101; Ungar, 96; Vine, 97, 101
Clayton, Paul, *Whaling and Sailing Songs from the Days of Moby Dick* (LP), xi
Clergymen, bad luck aboard ship, 12
Coins, superstitions associated with, 83–87
Compass, bad luck using one with an inverted needle, 6
Confidence-Man, ix–x, 26–27, 32, 34–36, 63–64
—chapters: Chapter 3, "In Which a Variety of Characters Appear," 34; Chapter 45, "The Cosmopolitan Increases in Seriousness," 34–35
Constitution ("Old Ironsides"), 2–3, 18, 84, 104–5; canes made from its timbers, 3, 90; wood from as charm, 2–3
Command, "the only way to learn to command is to learn to obey" (proverb), 31
Cooper, James Fenimore, *Red Rover,* 1
Copenhagen, 10
Corposants (St. Elmo's Fire), ix, 46–49, 90; as souls of dead sailors, 47; associated with suicide, 47; superstitions associated with, 48–49
Counterfeit Detector, 35
Crockett, Davy, 76, 80
Crucifix, tattoo of as charm, 4–5
Cruel, "cruel as a Turk" (proverbial comparison), 29

Daboll, Nathan: "according to Daboll" (proverbial phrase), 85; *Arithmetic,* 85–86

INDEX

Dana, Richard Henry, 38, 73; *Two Years Before the Mast*, 12, 71, 104

"Daniel Orme," 5

Darkness, "it's always darkest before the dawn" (proverb), 34

Dead Sea, x

Defoe, Daniel, *Robinson Crusoe*, 64

Delirium Tremens, 65–66

Devil, 2, 10; associated with wind (motif G303.6.3.3), 11, 84; must count grains of sands, 4

Direct discourse, 53–54, 56, 86

Dirt, magic as protection (motif D1380.9), 3

Divination, 68–71, 87

Doubloon, 83–87

Dreams, interpretation of, 68–71

Duyckinck, Evert, 75

Duyckinck, George, 77

Elizabeth, St., 102

Emerson, Ralph Waldo, 29; "Demonology," 41; *Essays*, 51; "Prudence," 51

"Encantadas," ix, 9, 14, 22–24, 31–32

Enderby, Samuel, 105

England, 14, 46

Erasmus, 27

Essex (ship), 78

Eteocles, 93

Europe, 10, 92

Famous Historie of Friar Bacon, 64, 76

"Far Off-Shore," 105

Father, "like father like son" (proverb), 25

Faust, 64, 76

Feathers: "fine feathers don't make fine birds" (proverb), 25; "Fine feathers on foul meat" (proverb), 26

Ferguson, James, *Astronomy*, 85

Fig, "to give a fig" (proverbial phrase), 25–26

"Figurehead," 105

Figurehead, supernatural power of, 3, 105

Fiji, 80

Fink, Mike, 76

Finland, 10

Finnish sailors: clairvoyance of, 2, 9–10, 40–41; supernatural powers of, 12, 104

Fire, body catches fire of its own accord (motif F964.3.3), 44

Flames, issue from a body's mouth (motif E421.3.7), 44

Flying Dutchman (motif E511), 38–39, 78, 106

Folk speech, x–xi. *See also* Proverbs

Folksongs, xi, 13–24. *See also* Ballads; Shanties; titles of specific songs

Folktales, xi, xi–xii, 51–61, 82. *See also* Tall tales

Fortunatus, 62

Fortune-telling, 10, 68–71, 87

Frank, Stuart M., xi

Franklin, Benjamin, 32–34, 66, 75, 80; *Poor Richard's Almanac*, 32–33; *The Way to Wealth*, 32–34, 63, 66

Franklin, H. Bruce, *The Wake of the Gods*, x

Fratricide, legends concerning, 93–94

Friday, bad luck associated with, 2–3, 18

Galileo, 98

Genette, Gérard, 53

Ghost stories, xi, 38–49

Ghosts, 3, 38–49; a moving figure in white mistaken for a ghost (motif J1782.6), 45

Gilman, Caroline Howard, *Oracles from the Poets*, 87

Gilman, Gorham Dummer, 93

God: "God goes 'mong the worlds blackberrying" (proverb), 86–87; "God helps them that help themselves" (proverb), 33

Goethe, 64, 76

Goldsmith, Oliver, *The Vicar of Wakefield*, 36

Goney bird (albatross): as soul of departed sailor, 9, 22, 106

INDEX

"Good Craft 'Snow-Bird,'" 26
Goose, "wild goose chase" (proverb), 34–36
Great Britain, 95
Greece, 92–93
Greene, Richard Tobias, 13, 52
Grobman, Neil, xii
Grose, Francis, 36
"Gumbo Squash" (folksong), 18
Guy of Warwick, 63

Hammock: as burial shroud, 39–40, 45; "white as a hammock" (proverbial comparison), 45
Handsome, "handsome is as handsome does" (proverb), 25, 36–37
Handwriting, as talisman, 67, 71–72
Harper's Classical Library, x
Harpoon iron, as talisman, 90–91
Hat, bad luck associated with, 7
Hatch, Agatha, 37
Hawaii, 59, 93
Hawthorne, Nathaniel, 37, 73, 77, 95
"Hawthorne and His Mosses," 64
Head, "to lose your head" (proverbial phrase), 30
Hemp, "to take a walk up Ladder-lane and down Hemp-street" (proverbial phrase), 31
Herod, 10
History of Blue Beard, 63
History of Dick Whittington and His Cat, 72–73, 75
History of Dr. Faustus, 76
History of Goody Two Shoes, 63–64
History of Sinbad the Sailor, 64
Hoadley, John C., 99, 102
Hoff, William, 104
Hoffman, Daniel, *Form and Fable in American Fiction,* ix–x
Holy Land, xiii, 92–103
Home Oracles, 87
Homer, 18, 94
"Hood's Isle and the Hermit Oberlus," 31–32, 44
Horseshoe: as supernatural medium,

40–41; for good-luck (motif D1561.1.3), 1; nailed to the mast for protection against harm (motif G272.11), 1, 84; stubbs have supernatural powers (motif G224.13.1), 89–90; tall tale about, 55
"Hugh of Lincoln" (ballad), 96–97
Humor, ix, xii, 4, 27, 29, 46, 51–61, 86. *See also* Lies; Tall tales
Hunt, Leigh, 38

"I and My Chimney," 26
Index Rerum, 25
Indirect discourse, 53, 55, 57
Initiation, 42, 54, 61
Iron, magic associations (motif D1252.1.1), 89. *See also* Harpoon; Horseshoe
Irony, 25–37, 41
Isle of the Cross, 37
Isle of Man, 10, 12, 80
Isle of Skye, 10
Israel Potter, xii, 6–7, 12, 32–34, 47–48, 62, 64, 66, 105
—characters: Benjamin Franklin, 32, 66; John Paul Jones, 7, 12, 33, 48, 66, 105; Israel Potter, xii, 7, 32–34
Italy, 92

Jack the Giant-Killer, 64
Jackson, Andrew, 3
Jerusalem, x, 92, 95, 97, 99
"Jim along Josey" (folksong), 18
"John Marr," 103–4
John Marr and Other Sailors, xiii, 103–7
Jones, Bartlett C., xii
Jones, John Paul, 7, 12, 33, 47, 66, 105
Jones, William, 59
Juan Fernández, 80

Kamchatka, 80
Kidd, Captain William, 65
King, Solomon, 52, 64
Koran, 66

Lansing, Kate Ganesvoort, 99

INDEX

INDEX

Murray, Lindley, *English Grammar,* 85–86
Mushabac, Janes, ix
Mythic criticism, x
Mythology, x, 7, 93

Nantucket, 3–4, 57–60, 80
"Nantucket Song," 20
Napoleon's Book of Fate, 67–71, 76, 79, 87
Negro Singers Own Song Book, 18
Nelson, Admiral Horatio, 1
New York, 25, 31, 65
New York Public Library, 64
Niagara Falls, 77
"Norfolk Isle and the Chola Widow,"
   22–24
Nukuheva, 13

Occult books, xii, 63, 67–71
Oedipus, 93
"Old Ironsides." See *Constitution*
"Old King Crow" (song), 87
Omens, ix, 1–2, 7–10, 22, 38, 41, 44, 47–
   49, 86, 88–89
Omoo, xi, 1, 10, 15–17, 20–21, 23, 26, 27,
   29–30, 39–41, 43–44, 54–58, 60, 81, 86
—characters: Dr. Long Ghost, x, 15, 30;
   Tonoi, 55, 57; Van, 40–41
"On the Coast of Barbaree" (folksong),
   15
Organs, human organs replaced with
   animals' (motif X1721.2), 57
Owens, Robert Dale, *The French
   Revolution,* 64

Parker, Hershel, *Herman Melville: A
   Biography,* xii
Patch, Sam, 76–77
Personal legend, xi, 39–40, 44, 86
Personal narrative, xi, 39–40
Phantom sailors, 38–49
Philo Logos Society, 41
Picture of Liverpool, 71–72
Pierre, x, 31, 34, 72
—characters: Delly, 31; Isabel, 31, 72;
   Pierre Glendinning, x, 31, 64
Pig: organs substituted for human's,

57; superstitious associations, 5–6;
   tattoo of as charm, 5
Pilot fish, as sign of good luck, 8
Poe, Edgar Allan, 39; *Narrative of
   Arthur Gordon Pym,* 52
Polynesia, 92
Polynices, 93
Pope, Alexander, 20
Porpoise, 58
Porter, William T., *Quarter Race in
   Kentucky,* 36
Potter, Israel, xii, 7, 32–34
Pride, "as proud as Lucifer" (proverbial
   comparison), 84
Printing, "to beat printing" (proverbial
   phrase), 35
Prometheus, 43
Proverbs, x–xi, 11, 25–37, 86; manufac-
   tured proverbs, 30; sailor proverbs,
   30–31. *See also* individual proverbs,
   proverbial phrases, and proverbial
   comparisons listed separately under
   key words
Psalms, 33
Pynchon, Thomas, *V,* 86

Rabelais, François, 20
Redburn, ix–x, xii, 11–12, 16–17, 20–22,
   26–27, 29–31, 42–44, 46, 48, 53–54,
   59, 62–77; Chapter 18, "He Endeav-
   ors to Improve His Mind; and Tells
   of One Blunt and His Dream–
   Book," 65–71
—characters: Jack Blunt, 11–12, 66–71,
   76, 79, 87; Jackson, 42–44; Mrs.
   O'Brien, 11–12; Wellingborough
   Redburn, 8, 21–22, 42–44, 53–54, 62–
   73, 76–77; Captain Riga, 26; Miguel
   Saveda, 42–44, 48
Remarkable Life of Dr. Faustus, 64
Reynard the Fox, 62
Rock, chunk of from St. Paul's Cave in
   Malta as charm against shipwreck, 2
Rome, 92, 100; "when at Rome do as
   the Romans do" (proverb), 28
Rooster, tattoo of as charm, 5

INDEX

Melville's Folk Roots

was designed and composed in 10½/12½ Adobe Minion

by Diana Dickson and Will Underwood

on an Apple Power Macintosh system using Adobe PageMaker

at The Kent State University Press;

printed by sheet-fed offset lithography

on 50-pound Glatfelter Supple Opaque Natural stock

(an acid-free recycled paper),

Smyth sewn and bound over binder's boards

in Arrestox B cloth, and wrapped with dust jackets

printed in two colors on Permalin Multicolor Scroll stock

by Thomson-Shore, Inc.;

and published by

The Kent State University Press

KENT, OHIO 44242 USA